THE EPIC OF
SON-JARA

Jeli Fa-Digi Sisòkò

THE EPIC OF *SON-JARA*

A West African Tradition

Notes, Translation, and
New Introduction by
John William Johnson

Text by
Fa-Digi Sisòkò

Transcribed and translated
with the assistance of
Charles S. Bird, Cheick Oumar Mara,
Checkna Mohamed Singaré, Ibrahim Kalilou Tèra,
and Bourama Soumaoro

INDIANA UNIVERSITY PRESS
Bloomington and Indianapolis

African Epic Series

THOMAS A. HALE AND JOHN W. JOHNSON, GENERAL EDITORS

First Midland Book Edition 1992

Manufactured in the United States of America

Library of Congress Cataloging-in-Publication Data

Johnson, John William, date.
The epic of Son-Jara : a West African tradition / notes, translation, and new introduction by John William Johnson ; text by Fa-Digi Sisòkò ; transcribed and translated with the assistance of Charles S. Bird . . . [et al.].—1st Midland Book ed.
p. cm.
Includes bibliographical references (p.).
ISBN 0-253-33102-1 (cloth).—ISBN 0-253-20713-4 (paper)
1. Keita, Soundiata, d. 1255, in fiction, drama, poetry, etc.
2. Epic of Son-Jara. I. Sisòkò, Fa-Digi. II. Epic of Son-Jara. English. III. Title.
PL8491.9.E63J6 1992
896′.34—dc20 91-27300

1 2 3 4 5 96 95 94 93 92

To Nathan and Sam

N'i fòra mògò dòlu kò,
Mògò dòlu de f'i kò!

As you succeeded some,
So shall you have successors!

Contents

ILLUSTRATIONS

PREFACE

The famous epic of Son-Jara (also known in West Africa as Sunjata, sometimes spelled Soundiata),[1] which celebrates the exploits of the legendary founder of the empire of Old Mali or Manden some 750 years ago, is widely recited today among the Mandekan-speaking peoples of West Africa. As performed by *griots,* or professional bards, it constitutes a virtual social, political, and cultural charter of society, embodying deep-rooted aspects of Mande cosmology and worldview. Comprising 3,084 lines of poetry, the text presented here is the first full linear translation of a performance of the Son-Jara epic recorded in its heartland, a four-hour recitation by the *griot* Fa-Digi Sisòkò in the town of Kita in west-central Mali. What is unique about this translation is that it is not *reconstructed* or "rewritten" in words chosen by a translator or editor. The linear translation in this text is a word-for-word rendition of the actual words of the *griot.* An introduction precedes the text, which is also followed by a full set of annotations that provide a historical and contextual framework for understanding the recitation of this still-living West African epic.

This translation first appeared as the second section of an analytical volume which included an extensive ethnographic study of the Mande peoples of West Africa, whose bards recite this epic in public.[2] The present edition provides an affordable volume of the epic text available to the public for a variety of uses. Teachers will find the book helpful for classroom use, and it will prove beneficial in various kinds of courses, at both the university and the high school levels, where epic texts are needed. Literary scholars who teach courses on the genre of epic will be pleased to have a readable, authentic, linear translation of one of the world's great epics. Folklore and anthropology scholars who study the social use of text-based traditions and oral literature will also appreciate the volume. Scholars of African written literature who like to begin their course with the flavor of oral performance will find this book inexpensive enough to include on their reading lists. And finally, those among the general public who enjoyed reading *Roots* will recognize Son-Jara's adversary Sumamuru Kantè (pronounced Kinte in Gambian Mandinka) as an early kinsman of Alex Haley. This text should be a welcomed contribution to the growing list of famous epics of world history. Becoming more and more publicized, the epic of Son-Jara (Sunjata) is taking its place alongside the great epics *Gilgamesh,* the *Iliad,* the *Odyssey, Beowulf,* the *Nibelungenlied,* the *Song of Roland,* the *Kalevala,* the *Ramayana,* the *Mahabharata,* and *El Cid.*

This text was collected on 9 March 1968, with a Nagra tape recorder, in the city of Kita in western Mali by Charles S. Bird, professor of linguistics at Indiana University. The performance lasted roughly four hours, from about 3:00 P.M. to about 7:00 P.M. The tapes became a part of the literary and linguistic data in Bird's vast collection and were not transcribed until 1973, Bird being involved in other projects in Malian studies. As a graduate student in folklore at Indiana University, with a grant from the Social Science Research Council, I set off with my family to conduct field research in Mali on the Son-Jara epic, and Bird turned the tapes over to me to take back to Mali for transcription, translation, and annotation. I also collected five other texts during this field project, all of which were involved in the overall process of analysis of this form of oral literature in Mali. The present text was transcribed and translated twice. It was initially transcribed in Mali by my assistant Cheick Oumar Mara. I executed the translation and extensive annotation with the help of two other Malian assistants, Ibrahim Kalilou Tèra and Checkna Mohamed Singaré. Later the text was again transcribed, by Bourama Soumaoro, and a second translation was accomplished in sessions involving Bird, Soumaoro, and me. The final translation constitutes a synthesis of the two series of work sessions.

Many people have given generously of their time and knowledge to make this book a reality, and it would be impossible to mention them all by name. Foremost on the list is the bard, Fa-Digi Sisòkò, who agreed to share his version of this great epic with us. All those involved in work on the text are to be thanked, and they take their rightful place on the title page. My gratitude is extended especially to Charles S. Bird for his long-standing encouragement of my work on West African epic. Thanks are also due to the Social Science Research Council for providing the major funding for my research project in Mali. All conclusions, statements, and opinions in the book are, however, mine, and not necessarily those of the SSRC or of anyone else involved. I appreciate the help of Indiana University, which provided a grant-in-aid for the purchase of equipment, and of M. Mamadou Sarr, the director of the Institut des Sciences Humaines du Mali when I was there.

My brief encounter with Magan Sisòkò, Fa-Digi's son, left a lasting impression, as he also sang a version of the epic which I published through the Folklore Students' Association at Indiana University. Magan taught me much about the epic and about his father. The premature death of Magan in an automobile accident shocked and grieved all of us who worked with him.

Five other people—my parents, Bill Johnson and my late mother, Tina; my parents-in-law Margaret Land and my late father-in-law, Victor; and my wife, Elizabeth—gave me much encouragement and assistance. Finally, I would like to express my sincere appreciation to the government and people of the Republic of Mali for permitting me and my family to live and work in their presence. They are among the friendliest and most hospitable people in the world, especially to the foreigner who has the good fortune to experience their ancient and fascinating culture.

Notes

1. The spelling of *Son-Jara* in this book follows the pronunciation of the Mandinka bard Fa-Digi Sisòkò, whose variant text is here translated. As a folklorist, I feel I should follow the traditions of the bard and not edit any of his pronunciations. The hero represented in this text is more widely known in scholarship as "Sunjata," though his name is spelled in various ways, usually reflecting the spelling conventions of the native language of the collector, and not those of the Mandekan language where the texts are collected. To complicate matters, Son-Jara also has a number of "praise-names," which celebrate his many exploits as a culture hero. For a detailed note on Son-Jara's various names and praise-names, see the note for line 1 following the text of the epic.

2. For a more detailed description and analysis of the context and performance of this text, see *The Epic of Son-Jara: A West African Tradition,* Analytical Study and Translation by John William Johnson (Bloomington: Indiana University Press, 1986).

Introduction

The Hero

Western and Western-trained scholars who attempt to reconstruct a chronological history of the great empire period of West Africa have argued that Son-Jara, or, as he is more widely known, Sunjata, was a historical person.[1] Unlike their predecessors whose theories were often unacceptable to scholars of oral literature, more recent oral historians have refined their methodologies in searching for the historicity in oral traditions by responding to sound criticism from functional and structural anthropologists. Far from being deterred by the criticism, these historians were inspired by it. They did not lose their faith in oral tradition as evidence of past history.

However refined the new methodologies of contemporary oral historians may be, the question of *what* Son-Jara represents today remains easier to answer than that of *who* he may have been 750 years ago in a land where historiography, or the writing down of history in the modern sense, did not appeal to people. The epic which celebrates his memory constitutes a social and political charter, reflective of cosmology and worldview in the modern world.

Mali has had a long and colorful history, producing many illustrious leaders. Several of them are celebrated in heroic literature, but none are paramount in Mande folklore to Son-Jara Keyta. His memory is recited in several genres wherever Mande languages are spoken (Mali, the Gambia, and portions of Senegal, Guinea-Conakry, Ivory Coast, and Mauritania). Kankan Musa, who ruled Mali from 1312 to 1327, is probably better known than Son-Jara outside Mali. It might be argued that Musa had a greater impact on the spread of knowledge about the empire of Old Mali to the outside world. His famous and ostentatious pilgrimage to Mecca in 1324–25, resulting in the dramatic inflation of the Egyptian gold standard economy, disseminated the name of Mali abroad to a greater degree than did Son-Jara's local exploits. Musa's pilgrimage went unmatched by any *mansa* ("emperor") before or after him; yet no epic among Mandekan speakers celebrates his exploits.

Son-Jara is the *mansa* most celebrated in oral narrative today, and it is to him that the society has assigned the role of *culture hero*. Indeed, many exploits of later *mansalu* have been telescoped into Son-Jara's lifetime, and, because of his status as hero, many accomplishments are attributed to him, no matter to whom historians credit these acts. The memory of him, as with most culture heroes, has been altered to conform to a heroic pattern. In this respect, folk belief holds a much stronger grip over the content of the epic recited about the hero than would any data to which documentation might lend proof.

For this and other reasons, the popularity of Son-Jara has outstripped that of the other *mansalu* of the empire of Old Mali. His memory is celebrated in a variety of narrative and other forms of folklore, including praise-poetry and prose legend. But it is in the epic that Son-Jara is fully glorified, for the epic is the most complex and celebrated form of oral literature to be found among Mandekan speakers.

It has been argued for over a hundred years that the description of a culture hero's life in heroic literature conforms to set patterns of behavior reflective of the society's worldview. Modern academic treatment of these patterns dates from von Hahn's treatise in 1876, which led to other, similar studies by Rank, Raglan, and de Vries.[2] Studying heroic life styles and plot motifs of culturally and historically related areas of Europe, the Middle East, and India, these scholars established lists of trait characteristics common to heroes, some lists more specific than others. Whatever other conclusions these scholars may have drawn from such an exercise, the evidence tended to suggest that heroes' lives conform to narrative stereotyping, again a characteristic which argues against the search for historicity in oral traditions.

The aforementioned scholars did not employ narratives about any African hero when they drew up their lists, because next to nothing had been published about African heroic narratives at the time they did their work. A deeper look into the heroic elements of the Mande hero, and other heroes of the African continent such as the Zulu warrior-king Shaka, reveals significant differences from their Indo-European counterparts, and a short description of Son-Jara's personality, stereotyped in epic performances, will be illustrated below.

The Bard

The performance of the epic of Son-Jara, and of many other epics in the Mande world, is carried out by professional raconteurs called *jeli,* or *jali* (*griot* in French). A description of the social system in which the bards live and participate will help us to understand the context of epic in this society. Bards are casted members of society, but they are not casted in the hierarchical sense of that term, as are members of Hindu society in India. To be casted in Mali is to have a protected socio-economic role; it is like belonging to a large and powerful labor union in Europe or the United States. The social roles of the bards must be described, for performing this important epic is only one of their several roles. Their training, various occupations, and economic orientation, as well as their monopoly over various performance modes, ensure them a secure role in society.

Throughout the Mande world there exists a group of clan families which can be described as castes. These families have the right to certain occupational pursuits, although they are not required to participate in their reserved specialties. They also have specifically defined social roles, and they practice endogamy to protect these roles. It must be made clear that Mande endogamous castes are not "despised," or hierarchical. They may be more correctly described as socio-economic monopolies, and not pecking orders. Several characteristics of Mande castes support these conclusions.[3]

Mande terminology would indicate social separation of these groups from the rest of society. The word *nyamakala* encompasses all casted families. Their roles, both economic and social, are hereditary, and their endogamy would seem to serve the function of preserving their monopoly over these roles and of avoiding competition to ensure that society runs smoothly. Their respective economic pursuits do not overlap. At least four groups exist in Mali and elsewhere in the Mande world: *numu* (blacksmiths, woodcarvers), *garangè* (leatherworkers), *funè* (mimes, Islamic praise-poets), and *jeli* (bards). Our interest here is with the *jeli*.

The economic role of the bards, like those of other casted groups, may be defined as monopolistic. All of their roles are concerned with the spoken word, and the power of their speech is considered more than merely entertaining or persuasive. It is a common belief that the power of the occult is conveyed in the bards' words, as is demonstrated vividly by the formula many people recite when giving gifts to bards after a performance:

> Ka nyama bò!
> *May the occult power be taken away!*

Although it cannot be denied that part of the bards' living is earned by the practice of oral art, Mande worldview considers payment for it to be a function of lessening the power that their words convey.

The bards' social roles are varied and complicated. One of the main roles is that of chronicler and, even more important, analyzer and interpreter of the history of the nation, economic group, and patron family (if he or she is so attached). The renowned Malian scholar Amadou Hampâté Bâ expressed this role in his statement that "with the death of each old man, a library is burnt."[4] On the other hand, one nation's history is interpreted as legend by another, and written forms of history are often complicated by social and nationalistic bias common at the time of its writing. Much of the bards' recitations must of necessity be considered favorable to their patrons. This reality helps explain characteristic changes and variations common to any oral tradition which is widespread over many regions.

A second role of the bard involves entertainment. The monopoly over musical instruments and certain genres of oral literature ensures the bards' artistic status. A third role is that of preserver of social customs and values. In this role, the bards' knowledge of "proper behavior" serves in the arena of social control. Bards often express opinions in public without fear of reprisal, though a bard I interviewed in Mali occasionally refused to answer some of my questions because, as he said, the information contained too much occult power. I came to realize later that this bard was from a different region of Mali and was uneasy about the reprisals locals might inflict on him for expressing dissenting views. Otherwise, the verbal liberty of bards is related to their endogamous separation from the lineage structure of the majority of Mande society, which underscores their fourth role.

The role of mediation is important and has many facets. As a seer, the bard acts as intercessor between the temporal and the spiritual. Bards often read divinations of various kinds and administer blessings and curses. They also serve as mediators between parties involved in some of the Mande rites of passage, such as Islamic naming ceremonies and marriages. Bards sometimes act as lineage spokespersons and take part in intervillage affairs as "ambassadors and conciliators."[5] Occasionally they perform valuable duties "in cases of serious rifts between two important families, where the impartiality of even the elders of the town might be questioned. . ."[6] Even where no rift is involved, a neutral agent is often needed, especially when there is a difference between the social status of the combatants. It is precisely because bards are outside the lineage structure that they can intervene without being suspected of personal involvement in the argument. Moreover, the bard often mediates between two parties so that they do not have to face each other and run the risk of angry confrontation.

In a role related to that of mediator, bards are sometimes responsible for initiating action. By praising or insulting a patron, the bard can move that person to act. This role is often mentioned in epic poetry, as are several others which are difficult to assess in modern times, because social conditions have changed. For instance, bards profess to have been the conscience of kings and to have moved them to action with their poetry. They claim to have followed warriors into battle, singing encouragement to enhance their bravery, and they allege to have been immune from warfare and slavery themselves. If captured, they purport to have been either released by their captors, or taken into their service as bards rather than as slaves. Considering their exclusion from lineage affairs in modern times, these boasts are not beyond possibility, but the evidence for their former status is now absent.

That bardic families were socially and economically allied to specific noble lineages in the past is well accepted in Mali today. That this socio-economic arrangement is no longer so widespread is also well attested. French colonialism changed many aspects of social and political life in Mali, and the older patron/protégé relationships are no exception. Before colonialism, bards enjoyed privileges and exercised certain duties with regard to the families to which they were allied. These families often provided home and food, as well as clothing and other necessities and luxuries of life.

Some degree of family attachment survives in Mandekan-speaking communities even today. Royal families are often replaced by merchant families, to whom many praise-poems are now directed. Not all royal families can afford patronage, but many merchants are wealthy enough to do so. One solution some bards have found is to "adopt more than one patron." Others take to the road as "free-lance griots" during the dry seasons.[7] Still another solution appears to be the adoption of an entire village as patron. Although I am not certain of this system, it appears to have been used in the case of the late bard Wa Kamisòkò of Kirina, a village southwest of Bamako. In addition to being spokesperson for the entire village, Wa earned some of his living as a farmer, an adaptation many bards have made. Indeed, some bards are quite successful as farmers, for they often have capital on hand to pay outside workers in their fields. The state provides patronage to a limited number of bards, but the competition is fierce. National troupes exist in Mali, Senegal, and Guinea, but they are periodically disbanded. The radio station provides some state assistance, but all of these varieties of patronage are irregular and can provide only partial income for most bards. Some bards today have adapted even more radically, playing in local youth and dance bands. Although adaptation has become necessary for the economic survival of the bardic caste, its social status appears in no danger of rapid radical change. The social roles of the bards are still intact.

Fa-Digi Sisòkò was a formal apprentice to his maternal uncle, and like his uncle, he became attached to an agricultural community.[8] Among many Sub-Saharan African farmers, work in the fields is done collectively. Sometimes the workers are members of the same age-set, and the entire group works on one plot at a time until all the fields are either sown or harvested. It is the responsibility of the host of the plot being worked to provide food and drink for the workers. Moreover, the host often provides for a bard who specializes in poetry concerning agricultural work and in directing the tempo or rhythm of farm labor. To strengthen his status, Fa-Digi attended at least one reroofing ceremony of the sacred hut in Kaaba (Kangaba). According to Mande traditions, Kaaba is considered the mythical center of the world and is certainly a cultural center of the multistate nation of Mandekan speakers. This ceremony is performed only once in every seven years and attracts crowds of people, many of them bards, from all over West Africa. One of the ceremony's highlights is a performance of the epic of Son-Jara by the Jabaatè bards from neighboring Kela, a recitation which lasts over several days (but only in the evenings). Fa-Digi's attendance at one of these recitals in Kaaba increased his prestige and gave him status as a bard acquainted with the "authentic" version of the epic.

The Text

The performance of the narrative of Son-Jara is classified as epic by folklorists who study genres of oral literature. Debates over how to define a genre, any genre, have occupied scholars for decades. Some contend that genres represent ethno-aesthetic constructs that only their users can define. Others take a more cross-cultural point of view, arguing that certain forms of oral literature are similar wherever they are found among human societies. No one epic tradition is identical to any other epic tradition, but the similarities of various examples of this generic form are so striking that I hold the latter view. I should like to suggest an underlying set of characteristics which might be used as a model for an academic construct of epic. All of the reliable variants of the epic of Son-Jara I have collected or read display these traits. Moreover, texts of epics from other parts of the world which I have read also exhibit these same traits, but the model which I would like to suggest is not merely based on textual analysis. Some of these traits could not have been isolated if only textual material had been analyzed. Fieldwork is necessary in order to gain a holistic picture of living epic traditions.

A holistic model of folk epic, then, should be based not only on structural considerations but also on contextual aspects of performance.

Structural characteristics include poetic language, narrative style, heroic content, great length, and multigeneric qualities. The contextual traits include legendary belief structure, multifunctionality, and cultural, traditional transmission. Let me give some detail about each of these traits.

Poetic Language

Epics are poems. Long heroic narratives in prose also exist among the world's societies, but academics refer to them as *sagas*. Indeed, some of the world's long heroic narratives exhibit traits of both poetry and prose. But epics are, by definition, poems. These long and complex poems are not memorized verbatim and reproduced word for word during each performance. They are created and recited at the same time. This form of formulaic performance[9] requires long years of study and practice by professional bards before they master the intricacies of prosody.

Sub-Saharan African prosodic systems, however, are not easy for the Western-trained scholar to decipher, because they are not based on any models that European languages employ in their poetry. In many scansion systems, accents or quantitative units may be analyzed separately from the pulses of possible musical accompaniment. It may be the case in parts of Sub-Saharan Africa that music and words are not separable from the total generic understanding, and the interaction of these two elements is necessary in order to know what the local population considers poetry. The British-born ethnomusicologist A. M. Jones calls such oral art "African metrical lyrics,"[10] where music and lyrics are inseparable. In other words, the generation of words is impossible without the actual or imagined rhythm generated by the musical accompaniment. The American linguist Charles S. Bird describes this system of prosody as characterized by *language-external constraints,* as opposed to the more usual Western poetry, the scansion of which is controlled by the text, or *language-internally constrained.*[11]

Mande epic, however, does not have only one scansion system. It has three, termed *modes,* each of which also has a literary function. The *narrative mode* tells the story. The *song mode* celebrates important narrative events in the plot. And the *praise-proverb mode* serves a role of transition between narrative scenes in the plot. Differing degrees of aesthetic tension arise between the singer and the musical accompaniment when melody and rhythm are combined in these modes.[12] In this text, praise-proverb mode is indented, and song mode is both indented and italicized.[13]

Narrative Style

Mandekan epics tell complicated stories, and their structures can be divided into three levels. First there is the *episode,* which groups together smaller units called *themes.*[14] Themes are divided further into yet smaller units made up of such elements as lines, motifs, genealogies, incantations, prayers, curses, oaths, pattern numbers, ideophones, praise-names, and proverbs.

The episodes are composed of groups of themes held together by their mutual relationships in the plot. The mutual relationships between the episodes are most often based on geographical place of action. The episodes in the text presented in this book, for example, take place in Paradise, Mecca, Sankaran (a city in the ancient land of Du), the Manden (Mali of old), Mèma (a city in what is now central Mali), Kulu-Kòrò (a city on the Niger near Bamako), and the Gambia. Although he is not consistent, Fa-Digi is fond of terminating his episodes with a proverb, which suggests movement from one place to another, signaling transition to a new episode:

Sigi tèna ko min ban,
Taama le o banna.

What sitting will not solve,
Travel will resolve.

Although these levels of structure may be isolated through a comparative method, there is no clear break in the performance of the epic. The bard continues singing without stopping once he has begun. It is possible to designate the exact line that divides themes, and praise-proverb and song modes are often employed to conjoin themes, but the bard does not stop his performance unless he calls for a break unrelated to the structure of the poem.

Heroic Content

In Mali, I often heard it said that Son-Jara was not like other men. At the same time, it was striking that his chief adversary, Sumamuru Kantè, was not despised. Indeed, the spirit of the latter is revered and worshiped in the town of Kulu-Kòrò (Kouloukoro) today. Clearly the contrast between Sumamuru and Son-Jara is not considered a question of good versus evil. There is a strong folk belief among many people in Mali that a hero—or anyone else, for that matter—has a destiny. This belief is not, however, one of predestination, for the hero must correctly identify and attempt to fulfill his appointed destiny. If he underestimates his capabilities and lacks ambition, he may lose his chances. If burning ambition drives him to advance too rapidly, he may be consumed by the occult power he needs in order to fulfill his destiny.

Although the hero may bring prestige and even wealth to his people, he is not so much admired personally as he is feared. For example, one major method the hero may employ to gain occult power (*nyama*), which is used to assist him in fulfilling his destiny, is to violate the tabus of society. If the hero is strong enough—that is to say, if he is in tune with his destiny at that stage of its fulfillment—he will be able to gain control over the occult power released by the violation and become even more powerful for the next step. If, on the other hand, he has attempted too much too fast, he may become consumed by the power.

The belief that political power is held not by force alone but by control of the occult, accounts for the themes which describe the paternal and maternal inheritances of Son-Jara. In this context, the Islamic concept of *barakah,* "grace," can be considered the Moslem equivalent of local Mande *nyama,* "occult power." From his father, descendant of immigrants from Mecca, Son-Jara inherits *barakah;* from his mother, descendant of the Buffalo-Woman of Du, he inherits *nyama.* With both of these occult sources, he will seek to gain the political power of his destiny. Son-Jara's major battles against his adversaries are described in the epic not as great conflicts of weaponry, but rather as battles of sorcery. But the inheritance of *barakah* and the personal acquiring of *nyama* are still not enough to provide Son-Jara with the power he needs to fulfill his destiny. Before Sumamuru can be defeated on the field of war, Son-Jara must first learn the secret of his occult power and make counter-sacrifices to eliminate its efficacy.

The heroic life of Son-Jara, the greatest of all Mandekan heroes, can be viewed as a series of transformations in the pursuit of power with which he is able to fulfill his destiny, according to Mandekan worldview. Beginning as a cripple, the limping hero goes through several transformations, each gaining him more power than the last, and finally he becomes the most powerful hero ever to have lived.

Great Length

Great length is a trait of Mandekan epic, but it is relative only to the other forms of oral folklore in the single society being studied. If we compare epic to its closest "cousin" in Mandekan folklore, the praise-poem, we can say that panegyrics are, in general, shorter than epics, the latter sometimes lasting several hours. When recorded and transcribed, with poetic lines demarcated and numbered, it can be said that praise-poems may be measured in hundreds of lines, while epics may be measured in thousands.

One interesting point concerning length, which is often measured by scholars who have studied epic, is that the narrative is open-ended. Skilled bards employ various techniques in order to lengthen or shorten the performance of the text, a trait I propose to call the *accordion effect.* Closely resembling De Vries's "theory of swelling,"[15] the former term would also encompass a theory of shrinking as well, for both occur in epics.

Multigeneric Qualities

Portions of the epic of Son-Jara can be isolated as separate genres that occur in Mande society. The epic as a whole constitutes a genre, since its structure, context, and functions are well defined, but the same can be said of the smaller generic forms embedded within it when they occur separately. This multigeneric structure is an important defining characteristic of this form of oral folklore.

Among the more complex forms are at least four varieties found as performance genres in Mande society. Legend, of course, occurs elsewhere in poetic and prosaic form. Genealogy recitation also occurs, as do songs and praise-poems, which are performed separately and in conjunction with other genres. Among the simpler generic forms are praise-names, folk etymologies, proverbs, incantations, curses, blessings, and oaths. The blending together of these various forms produces a generic form the sum of which is greater than its parts.

Legendary Belief Structure

Concerning the legendary characteristic, there is no question that the Mande populations of West Africa consider Son-Jara a historical personage. Because the pattern of his life has been molded to conform to a heroic pattern, however, the epic about this monarch can be described as legendary. Any given variant will contain many legends, and it is safe to say that, in the variants I collected, the etiological legend, often supported by a genealogy, is the most common variety. Many are embedded in episodes of the epic of Son-Jara. They are extremely important, for they play a major role in the bard's attempt to give order to the social behavior of Mande society.

Multifunctionality

The professional bard, as well as his audience, employs the epic for a variety of social functions. One of the major functions has remained at least partially intact in the midst of social and political change since the early days of colonialism, when this epic was first studied by foreigners. Although it is difficult, if not impossible, to gauge the degree to which the epic provides a model for the relations between clan families, Nicholas Hopkins has described how clan relations in Kita are modeled after those of the town's ancestors described in the epic of Son-Jara and in other legends concerned only with Kita.[16] It is important to take into account that there are variations in the interpretation of these relations over time and space. It is, moreover, hard to gauge the degree of social constraint and pressure on any individual bard and the degree of his personal integrity in describing what he believes to be the truth.

Professional segments of society, often cast as family monopolies, find an etiological sanction for their roles in epic. The freeman, bard, farmer, leatherworker, boatman, holy man, descendant of former slave or orphan, stranger, and many other members of society, all find their roles interpreted by bards, although it must also be said that bards do not always agree with each other. What is certain is that bards tend to describe society as they believe it ought to be rather than as it may actually be. The function is, therefore, more didactic than reflective in this respect.

Perhaps one of the most important functions of the epic of Son-Jara is its role in the national unity of the Mandekan-speaking peoples. Because of its detail on the common origin of widely dispersed clan families and ethnic groups, this epic plays a definitive role in building a sense of national identity, in spite of the fact that political boundaries drawn by French and British colonial powers persist in dividing these peoples. Nowhere is the national unity function exemplified and stressed more dramatically than in the reroofing festival of the sacred Mande hut in the village of Kaaba (Kangaba) mentioned earlier.

Finally, some functions of epic may be described as more or less parallel to those of the bard, for the epic is the property of the bardic families. As the bard is the chronicler of history (legend), so the epic is considered the chronicle of the Mande. As the bard sees himself as the preserver of social customs and values, so the epic becomes the catalogue of those customs and values.

Cultural, Traditional Transmission

Considered the official "protector" of culture, the professional casted bard who performs the epic of Son-Jara often sings about multifarious aspects of his society, such as material objects, foodstuffs, marriage customs, types of divination and occult medicine, and a host of other catalogues reflecting, or at least attempting to demonstrate, the bard's extensive knowledge of his cultural traditions. It would seem obvious that such a long narrative would mirror the culture from which it arose, but there may also be reasons for these vast catalogues.

Constant reinforcement of cultural data may well serve as an enculturating force on its audience. Moreover, the bard often enhances his own prestige by including so much unsolicited information and description. Akin to name dropping, this practice strengthens his credibility in a society where there are many competing bards.

Extreme caution must be exercised while searching the lines of any epic for such data. There is a danger in trusting internal evidence without verification through firsthand fieldwork. Often parts of the narrative are employed for literary purposes only, and bards are opinionated persons who can hold points of view at variance with those of the majority of society. At the same time, epics are indeed filled with descriptions and catalogues of cultural information useful to those wishing to understand the remarkable society from which this famous epic has emerged.

Résumé of the Plot

Because the plot of the epic is extremely detailed, a résumé of the themes is useful. The description of the plot listed below is preceded by the line number on which the theme begins.

Line Theme

1 Prologue: Praise-poem.
56 Satan cast out of Paradise.
126 God places Adam on the earth.
154 Genealogy of Adam's family.
160 Genealogy of Noah's family.
175 Genealogy of Jòn Bilali's family.
182 Founding of the Manden and the populating of its regions; composition of its clan families.
242 Genealogy of the three Simbon brothers.
289 Genealogy of the Taraweres.
325 Genealogy of the Kòndès.
356 The breach of faith between Sankaran Naminya Kòndè and Du Kamisa.
461 Hunters try to kill the buffalo of Du but fail.
466 The Tarawere brothers are prepared by occult means.
527 The Tarawere brothers seek out the Buffalo-Woman and learn her secrets.
635 The Tarawere brothers overcome the Buffalo-Woman.
749 Origin of the Jabaatè clan.
752 Genealogy of the Jabaatès.
916 The brothers receive Sugulun Kòndè as their reward.
947 The Tarawere brothers try to lie with Sugulun Kòndè, but she turns them away with occult power.
1027 Fara Magan, the Handsome, King of the Manden, gets Sugulun Kòndè from the Tarawere brothers.
1048 Son-Jara and King Dankaran Tuman are born and announced; origin of their rivalry.

1123 Son-Jara receives his first praise-name at birth.
1151 King Dankaran Tuman's mother hexes Son-Jara and makes him crippled.
1160 Son-Jara makes the ḥājj with the aid of a jinn.
1178 The battle of the rams.
1199 Son-Jara gets a counter-sacrifice dog; the battle of the dogs.
1290 Sugulun Kòndè seeks baobab leaves from her neighbors but fails to get any.
1403 Son-Jara stands up and walks.
1460 Son-Jara gains praise-names at the sacred baobab tree.
1476 Son-Jara revenges his mother's damaged honor by uprooting the baobab tree and carrying it to her compound.
1536 Son-Jara becomes a great hunter and gives up his claim to the throne.
1647 King Dankaran Tuman's mother makes him send Son-Jara into exile.
1689 Son-Jara seeks refuge with Jobi Kònatè, the Seer, but must go farther afield to escape his brother's wrath.
1716 Son-Jara seeks refuge with the Magasubaa King Tulunbèn of Kòlè.
1725 King Tulunbèn of Kòlè sacrifices an unborn child to Son-Jara's fetish and is punished by God.
1768 Son-Jara seeks refuge with the nine Queens-of-Darkness, who steal his wraith.
1778 King Dankaran Tuman sends Dòka, the Cat, and his daughter to Sumamuru.
1866 Origin of the Kuyatè clan.
1875 Genealogy of the Kuyatès.
1880 Sumamuru conquers the Manden.
1893 The origin of the Kisis.
1905 Sumamuru puts calabashes over the mouths of the Manden's heroes.
1925 Son-Jara regains his wraith from the nine Queens-of-Darkness by giving them nine buffaloes.
2037 Son-Jara goes to seek refuge with Prince Tunkara in Mèma.
2127 Mèma Sira instructs Son-Jara on the correct wording of the *sigi*-game.
2199 Son-Jara plays the *sigi*-game with Prince Tunkara of Mèma.
2232 Son-Jara's sister, Sugulun Kulunkan, takes the calabashes off the mouths of the Manden's heroes.
2238 Son-Jara is sought by people from the Manden, who locate his family by offering Manden products in the Mèma market.

2272 Son-Jara's sister, Sugulun Kulunkan, extracts the livers and hearts from the hunters' kill and offers them as guest food to the visitors from the Manden; Manden Bukari objects and a battle of sorcery follows. Manden Bukari is cursed by his sister.
2410 Son-Jara sacrifices shea-butter to one of his fetishes.
2449 Son-Jara's mother dies as an omen to his coming to power.
2466 Son-Jara threatens Prince Tunkara of Mèma in order to get land to bury his mother.
2556 Son-Jara tears off the Dabò's head in anger; origin of the Dabò clan.
2576 Son-Jara's army is carried across the Niger River by the Boatman after Son-Jara reveals his identity to him.
2632 Son-Jara attacks Sumamuru several times, but his occult is not strong enough; he retires and founds towns in the Manden.
2668 Son-Jara's sister, Sugulun Kulunkan, seduces Sumamuru and learns his sacrifice secrets.
2746 Sumamuru steals Fa-Koli's only wife; Fa-Koli joins Son-Jara.
2770 Fa-Koli makes the counter-sacrifices destroying Sumamuru's occult power.
2828 Sumamuru is pursued to Kulu-Kòrò and defeated; he becomes the sacred fetish there.
2909 Son-Jara rescues the bard Bala Faseke Kuyatè.
2949 Messengers are sent to the Land of Jolof to purchase horses; they are expelled and Son-Jara is insulted.
3000 Tura Magan buries himself in his own grave in order to have the army placed under his command.
3051 Tura Magan conquers the Gambia and other lands for the empire.

Notes

1. To learn more about the history of Mali and of Son-Jara's role in it, see J. Spencer Trimingham's *A History of Islam in West Africa* (London: Oxford University Press, 1970).

2. The four principal books which have made systematic studies of the heroic traits of Indo-European culture heroes are Johann Georg von Hahn, *Sagwissenschaftliche Studien* (Jena: F. Mauke [E. Schenk], 1876); Otto Rank, *The*

Myth of the Birth of the Hero (New York: Vintage, 1959; first published as *Der Mythus von der Geburt des Helden* [Leipzig and Vienna: F. Deuticke, 1909]); Lord Fitz Roy Richard Raglan, *The Hero: A Study in Tradition, Myth, and Drama* (London: Watts, 1949; first published in 1936); and Jan de Vries, *Heroic Song and Heroic Legend* (London: Oxford University Press, 1963).

3. Conclusions from my field experience concerning the socio-economic roles of casted families in Mali are supported by others who have worked with bards. For other opinions concerning the roles of the bard in Mande society, see Charles S. Bird, "Oral Art in the Mande," in *Papers on the Manding,* ed. Carleton T. Hodge (Bloomington: Indiana University Press and Research Center for the Language Sciences, 1971), pp. 15–26; Seni Darbo, *A Griot's Self-Portrait: The Origins and Role of the Griot in Mandinka Society as Seen from Stories Told by Gambian Griots* (Banjul: Gambian Cultural Archives, 1976); Nicholas S. Hopkins, "Mandinka Social Organization," in *Papers on the Manding,* pp. 99–128; Lilyan Kesteloot, "The West African Epics," *Présence Africaine* 30:58 (1966): 197–202; and Bokar N'Diayé, *Les Castes au Mali* (Bamako: Édition Populaire, 1970).

4. Quoted from Kesteloot, "The West African Epics," p. 202.

5. N'Diayé, *Les Castes au Mali,* p. 49.

6. Darbo, *A Griot's Self-Portrait,* p. 11.

7. Darbo, *A Griot's Self-Portrait,* pp. 12–15.

8. I gathered information about Fa-Digi Sisòkò primarily from his son, Jeli Magan Sisòkò, whom I interviewed in 1974.

9. For a description of formulaic methods of composition, see A. B. Lord, *The Singer of Tales* (New York: Atheneum, 1971). For a more detailed analysis of the formulas in the epic of Son-Jara, see John William Johnson et al., *The Epic of Son-Jara: A West African Tradition* (Bloomington: Indiana University Press, 1986).

10. A. M. Jones, "African Metrical Lyrics," *African Language Studies* 5 (1964): 52–63.

11. See Charles S. Bird, "Aspects of Prosody in West African Poetry," in *Current Trends in Stylistics,* ed. Braj B. Kachru and Herbert F. W. Stahlke (Edmonton, Alberta: Linguistic Research, 1972), pp. 207–15; and also "Poetry in the Mande: Its Form and Meaning," *Poetics* 5 (1976): 89–100.

12. For a more detailed description of the modes in the epic of Son-Jara, see Johnson et al., *The Epic of Son-Jara.*

13. Another stylistic practice in this text needs explanation. Often an apprentice, the naamu-sayer (*naamunaamuna*), shouts the word *naamu* (from Arabic *na'am,* "yes") and other encouraging words after most lines of the narration in order to stimulate the mastersinger. The words in parentheses after Fa-Digi's lines in the body of the text are the naamu-sayer's pronouncements.

14. For a description of themes in epic, see Lord, *The Singer of Tales.*

15. De Vries, *Heroic Song and Heroic Legend,* pp. 260ff.

16. Nicholas Hopkins, "Mandekan Social Organization," in *Papers on the Manding,* p. 101. Two other works also draw attention to the function of epic as a model for clan relations. They are Charles S. Bird, "The Development of Mandekan (Manding): A Study of the Role of Extra-linguistic Factors in Linguistic Change," in *Language and History in Africa,* ed. David Dalby (London: Frank Cass, 1971), p. 157; and Gordon Innes, *Sunjata: Three Mandinka Versions* (London: School of Oriental and African Studies, University of London, 1974), pp. 32–33.

Jeli Fa-Digi Sisòkò and His Wives

Jeli Fa-Digi Sisòkò with His Wives and His Naamunaamuna

Priest Standing before the Sacred Hut in Kangaba

Kulubali Priest and Sumamuru's Fetish (Nyanan) in Kulu-Kòrò

Nyanan: Fetish and Sacrificial Implements

The Epic

Episode One: Prologue in Paradise

Nare Magan Kònatè!
Sorcerer-Seizing-Sorcerer!
A man of power is hard to find.
And four mastersingers. [?] (Indeed)
O Kala Jula Sangoyi!
Sorcerer-Seizing-Sorcerer! (Mmm)

It is of Adam that I sing.
Of Adam,
Ben Adam. ('Tis true)
As you succeeded some,
So shall you have successors!
It is of Adam that I sing, of Adam. (Indeed)

I sing of Biribiriba! (Indeed)
Of Nare Magan Kònatè!
Sorcerer-Seizing Sorcerer! (True)
From Fatiyataligara
All the way to Sokoto, (Indeed)
Belonged to Magan Son-Jara. (Indeed)
Africans call that, my father,
The Republic of Mali, (Indeed)
The Maninka realm: (Mmm, 'tis true)
That's the meaning of Mali.
Magan Son-Jara,
He slayed Bambara-of-the-Border;
Settling on the border does not suit the weak. (Indeed)
And slayed Bambara-the-Lizard;

No weak one should call himself lizard. (Indeed)
And slayed Bambara-of-the-Backwoods;
Settling the backwoods does not suit the weak. (Indeed)
All this by the hand of Nare Magan Kònatè.
Sorcerer-Seizing-Sorcerer!
Simbon, Lion-Born-of-the-Cat. ('Tis true)

I sing of Biribiriba. (Indeed)
Stump-in-the-Dark-of-Night!
Should you bump against it,
It will bump against you. (Indeed)
Granary-Guard-Dog. (Indeed)
The thing discerning not the stranger,
Nor the familiar.
Should it come upon any person,
He will be bitten! (Indeed)
Kirikara Watita! (Indeed)
Adversity's-True-Place! (Indeed)
Man's reason and a woman's are not the same. (Indeed)
Pretty words and truth are not the same. (Indeed)
Almighty God created Adam, (Indeed)
Nine Adams. (Indeed)
The tenth one was Ben Adam. (True)

Ah, Bèmba! (Indeed)
Almighty God created Adam, the forefather, (Indeed)
And caused him to stand upon the earth,
And said that all creation's beings should submit to him.
And all the beings of creation did submit to him, (Indeed)
Save Iblis alone.
May God deliver us from Satan! (Amen, O my Lord)

Almighty God declared, "Iblis! (Indeed)
"If you do not submit to Adam, (Indeed)
"I will make you wretched. (Mmm)
"He is the last of all the Adams." (True)
Iblis replied, "My Lord, (Indeed)
"I'll not submit to Adam. (Indeed)
"For eighty years,
"I've taught the angels. (Indeed)
"Not one hand span, have I traveled o'er the earth, (Indeed)
"Where I did not submit to you. (Indeed)

"O God, reward me for all this." (Indeed)
"So be it," the reply. (Indeed)
"I will reward you. (Indeed)
"Ne'er will you catch disease. (Indeed)
"Ne'er your memory will fail. (Indeed)
"Ne'er will you need to sleep,
"Until the day the trumpet blows for man.
"Whosoe'er you lead astray,
"Among the next world's chosen will
not be." (Ah, Fa-Digi,
That's the truth)

And Iblis replied, "My Lord,
"Reward me still!" (Indeed)
"I will reward you," the reply. (Indeed)
"I will create a thing for your reward.
"I will create something just for you,
"And call it 'wealth.' "
"But the name of wealth should not be 'Wealth.'
"Call it the Voice of Transgression." (Indeed)
The Voice of Transgression: (Indeed)
Should man obtain it, (Indeed)
All his kin will he mistake. (Indeed)
And should man want of it,
'Tis he mistaken by his kin.
Its name is thus, the Voice of
Transgression. (That's the truth)
These six lines it addresses to its keeper: (Indeed)
"O My Keeper! (Indeed)
"Should I not be finished before you,
"You will be finished before me, my Keeper.
"If with this world I do not meld you, (Indeed)
"From this world I will divorce you. (Indeed)
"And if I get you not to Heaven, (Indeed)
"Then I'll send you down to Hell." (Indeed)
May God preserve us from these
people! (Amen, my Lord)
Almighty God then spoke, (Indeed)
"Adam! what may I offer you in life?" (True)
"O Lord," the reply, (Indeed)
"Give me beauty, O God." (Indeed)
"Adam, you are not the first to ask. (Indeed)

"It's to the jinns that I've given beauty, Adam." (Indeed)

Almighty God then asked,
"Now what may I offer to you?" (Indeed)
"O Lord," the reply, (Mmm)
"Give me morality, O God." (Indeed)
"Adam, you are not the first to ask. (Indeed)
"It's to the angels I've given morality, Adam." (Indeed)

Then Adam, our forefather, said, "O God, (Indeed)
"Whatever man may offer man, such will have
an end. (Indeed)
"Whatever God may offer man, no gift need follow that.
"Whatever you will give to me,
"That is what I wish." ('Tis the truth)
"Adam," the reply, (Indeed)
"I will grant you dignity.
"And how will you come to know
"That I did grant you dignity?
"Not as angel will Muhammad the Prophet be, (Indeed)
"Nor will I create him as a jinn.
"I will make him of Adam's seed." (Indeed)
Filardi Samawaati. [?]
Paradise and Earth were made according to His Love.
. . . (Indeed)
Where we have passed the day in Grace,
There may we also pass the night,
Amen. (Amen, O my Lord)

Ah! Bèmba! (Indeed)
Almighty God, after all of this, my father,
took Adam (Indeed)

And brought him forth from Paradise. (Indeed)
He set him down in a land, (Indeed)
The name of which was India. (Indeed)
Ask the ones who know of this!
Adam was placed in the land of India. (Mmm)
The land from whence the sun arises.
The land from whence the moon arises. (Indeed)
'Twas God who created the sun, (Indeed)
With its three hundred paths and thirty paths

And three paths, (Indeed)
And created the moon, (Indeed)
Three hundred paths and thirty paths and three paths. (Indeed)
When the sun leaves its path (Indeed)
To sit in the path of the moon, (Indeed)
When its light falls behind the moon, (Indeed)
The people cry out saying,
"The cat has seized the moon!"
The cat has not caught the moon. (Indeed)
The light of the sun is but behind it. (Indeed)
Our grandparent Eve and our ancestor Adam, (Indeed)
They sought each other out, (Indeed)
For forty days, (Indeed)
They were seeking for each other. (Indeed)
The mount whereon they met,
Its name was Arafan. (True)
Ask the ones who know of this! (True. That's true, Fa-Digi.)

Our grandparent Eve and our ancestor Adam, (Indeed)
Conceived some forty times, (Mmm)
And begat eighty children!
Ben Adam, (Indeed)
His first grandchild was Noah, (Indeed)
And he had three sons.

Episode Two: Mecca

Ah! Bèmba! (Indeed)
Noah begat three sons: (Indeed)
Ham, Shem, and Japheth. (Indeed)
Japheth went forth and crossed the sea. (Indeed)
His descendants became the Masusu and the Masasa. (Indeed)
Ham, black people descended from him, my father. (Indeed)
Shem, the twelve white clans (Indeed)
Descended from him. (Indeed)

I sing of Biribiriba! (Indeed)
Kirikisa, Spear-of-Access, Spear-of-Service! (Indeed)

The Messenger of God, Muhammad, was born, (Indeed)
On the twelfth day of the month of Dònba. (Indeed)
On the thirteenth day,
Tuesday, Bilal was born in Samuda. (Indeed)
Ask the ones who know of this! (Mmm)
That Bilal, (Indeed)
His child was Mamadu Kanu.
That Mamadu Kanu, (Mmm)
He had three sons: (Indeed)
Kanu Simbon, (Indeed)
Kanu Nyògòn Simbon,
Lawali Simbon. (Indeed)
Ah! Bèmba! (Indeed)
The races of man were ninety in number. (Indeed)
There were twelve clans of Marakas (Indeed)
Which came from Wagadugu. (Indeed)
The Sises came from Wagadugu. (Mmm)
The Janes came from Wagadugu. (Mmm)
The Tures came from Wagadugu. (Indeed)
The Beretes came from Wagadugu. (Indeed)
The Sakòs came from Wagadugu.
The Fulani came from Wagadugu. (Indeed)
The Jawaras came from Wagadugu. (Indeed)
The Nyarès came from Wagadugu. (Indeed)
The Tunkaras came from Wagadugu. (Mmm)

The peoples of Wagadugu thus scattered. (Indeed)
O Bèmba! (Indeed)
The ancestor of the Jawaras, Damangile, (Indeed)
And the forefather of the Nyarès, Nyenemba
Nyarè, (Indeed)
Went forth to found a village in Kingi. (Indeed)
The name of that village was Bambagile. (Indeed)
Damangile's tomb is there in Bambagile. (Indeed)
He had two children: (Indeed)
Daman and Sila Maan. (Indeed)
They both went forth to Jala. (Mmm)
Mount Siman and Mount Wala belong to the Jawaras
in Jala. (That's true)

Ah! Bèmba! (Indeed)
The ancestor of the Tunkaras, Prince Burama, (Indeed)

He went forth to found the village called Mèma. (Indeed)
There he had two sons, (Indeed)
Prince Burama and Jasigi. (Indeed)
Prince Burama and Jasigi, (Indeed)
'Twas they who joined Son-Jara here, (Indeed)
And went with him to the Manden. (Indeed)
They left the Manden later (Indeed)
And came to settle in Kulun. (Indeed)
They left Kulun, (Indeed)
And settled in Bangasi, (Indeed)
And went up on Genu Mountain, (Indeed)
And founded a village atop the mountain. (Indeed)
That village's name was Kuduguni. (Mmm, that's true)

'Tis said the Tunkaras of Genu, (Indeed)
They each had two sons: (Indeed)
Wali and Gayi, (Indeed)
Sega and Marama, (Indeed)
The four Tunkara patriarchs (Indeed)
Who were in Kita country here. (Indeed)
That is what those people are called. (True)

I sing of Biribiriba!
Kirikisa, Spear-of-Access and Spear-of-Service! (Mmm)
Warlord and wailing at his entry, a pile of stone!
Nare Magan Kònatè, Sorcerer-Seizing-Sorcerer! (Indeed)
Simbon, Lion-Born-of-the-Cat! (Indeed)

That Kanu Simbon and Kanu Nyògòn Simbon, (Indeed)
Settled in Wagadugu. (Indeed)
They left Wagadugu, (Indeed)
And they went to Jara. (Indeed)
They left Jara. (Mmm)
And went forth to found a farming hamlet, (Mmm)
Calling that village Farmtown. (Indeed)
That Farmtown is Manden Kiri-kòròni. (Indeed)
The very first Manden village was Manden Kiri-koroni. (Indeed)

Kanu Simbon, Kanu Nyògòn Simbon and Lawali Simbon, (Indeed)

Their first village was Manden Kiri-koroni, (Indeed)
Kiri-koroni! (Indeed)
Kanu Simbon, (Indeed)
He is the forefather of the Dankòs. (Indeed)
Lawali Simbon, (Indeed)
Begat Kòròlen Fabu and Sòkòna Fabu.
The Dugunòs descended from them. (Indeed)
Kanu Nyògòn Simbon (Indeed)
Begat King Bèrèmu, (Mmm)
King Bèrèmu begat King Bèrèmu Dana. (Indeed)
King Bèrèmu Dana begat King Juluku, the Holy. (Indeed)
King Juluku, the Holy begat King Belo Komaan. (Indeed)
Belo Komaan begat Juruni Komaan.
Juruni Komaan begat Fata Magan, the Handsome.
That Fata Magan, the Handsome (Indeed)
Went forth to found a farm hamlet called Kakama, (Indeed)
And they call that place, my father, Bintanya
Kamalen. (Mmm)
O Nare Magan Kònatè!
O Sorcerer-Seizing-Sorcerer! (Indeed)

That Fata Magan, the Handsome,
He married the daughter of
Tall Magan Berete-of-the-Ruins,
Called Saman Berete, the Pure. (Mmm)
They called her Saman Berete. (Indeed)
She had not yet borne a child at first. (Indeed)

O! Bèmba! (Indeed)
'Tis of the Manden!
There once were three and thirty noble clans.
In the Manden country:
Sixteen of warriors, (Indeed)
Four were agents of Dark Secrets, (Indeed)
Five were descendants of Mamuru, (True)
Five clans of holymen, (Indeed)
And four were families-that-came-later, (Indeed)
And one clan was of pariahs. (That's true,
Eh, Fa-Digi, true)

And five families of Mamuru: (Indeed)
King-of-the-Mountain, King-of-the-Clan, (Mmm)
Fa-banjugu and Wasa Kubari (Indeed)

And Sinunsi. (Indeed)
Those were the families of Mamuru.
Five families of holymen: (Indeed)
Tall Magan Berete-of-the-Ruins, (Indeed)
Seri Bukari Jane, (Mmm)
Sira Maan of the Ture Clan, (Mmm)
And Jabi Sise,
And Fodele, the Tall.
It was they who prayed to God in the Manden. (Indeed)

Ah! Bemba! (Indeed)
In our chronicles, (Mmm)
It was written in this way, my father, (Mmm)
Amongst the Arabs: (Indeed)
Among the Quraysh and Hāshim, (Indeed)
ʿAbd al-Muṭṭalib was the forefather of the Hāshim Clan. (Indeed)
ʿAbd al-Muṭṭalib begat ʿAbdullāh. (Indeed)
ʿAbdullāh begat Muḥammad. (Indeed)
Muḥammad begat Fatimah Bint. (Indeed)
Fatimah Bint (Indeed)
Gave birth to al-Ḥasan and al-Ḥusayn. (Indeed)
Al-Ḥasan, (Indeed)
The Sharīfs descended from him. (Indeed)
Al-Ḥusayn, (Indeed)
It was he who begat Abdulayi. (Mmm)

Abdulayi,
Could see in front
And see behind. (Indeed)
The name they gave him was Tarawara,
"The man of two visions." (True)
That is the meaning of being Tarawere. (Indeed)

That Abdulayi Tarawere, (Indeed)
Begat thirty sons. (Indeed)
They all fought the Kayibara battle for the Messenger of God (Indeed)
And they all remained on that field of battle, (Indeed)
All save Tukuru and Gasinè. (Indeed)
Tukuru and Gasinè, (Indeed)
The five holy families prayed to God
For Tukuru and Gasinè. (Indeed)

Both of them, (Indeed)
They each had one son. (Mmm)
It was they who became Dan Mansa Wulandin
And Dan Mansa Wulanba. (Mmm)
    The One-Who-Enters,
    The New-Year-Ram, Tura Magan!
    Tura Magan-and-Kanke-jan! (Ah, Fa-Digi, that's true)

Map of the Manden (Old Mali) and Surrounding Kingdoms At the Time the Epic of Son-Jara Takes Place (Modern State Boundaries Shown for Reference)

Episode Three: Sankaran

O! Bèmba! (Indeed)
We have come to the Jaras of Sankarandin. (Indeed)
To Naminya Kòndè of Sankaran.
The Kòndè's ancestor was Sama Sine. (Indeed)
Sama Sine was Aba Sara's child,

And it was he who begat Sana Bunuma Sara. (Mmm)
Sana Bunuma Sara (Indeed)
Bore her first son. (Indeed)
Sana Bunuma Sara, (Indeed)
Her first son was Leader-of-the-People. (Indeed)
That Leader-of-the-People, (Indeed)
His flesh-and-blood sister was Du Kamisa. (Mmm)
That Leader-of-the-People (Indeed)
Had a son called Magan Jata Kòndè of Du. (Indeed)
That Magan Jata Kòndè of Du, (Indeed)
At the shaving of his new-born hair, (Indeed)
His father's sister took that birth-hair,
And put it in a calabash,
Saying, "A thing for tomorrow!" (Indeed)

The umbilical cord that was cut,
She put into the calabash,
Saying, "A thing for tomorrow!"
The knife she used to cut the cord,
She put into the calabash,
Saying, "A thing for tomorrow!" (True)
His old swaddling cloth, (Mmm)
She put into the calabash, (Indeed)
Saying, "A thing for tomorrow!" (Indeed)
That small child grew up,
And came to rule over twelve towns.
All those people belonged to him.
He sought the counsel of wise men, (Indeed)
And they performed divination for him, (Indeed)
Saying that he must sacrifice a white spotted bull, (Mmm)
That an outsider should not eat of the meat.
And that was the aunt on the outskirts.
Living with an elder brother is not good. (Indeed)

Biribiriba, you and the bush!
O Nare Magan Kònatè!
'Tis of the Sorcerer I sing. (Indeed)
Kirikisa, Spear-of-Access and Spear-of-Service! (Mmm)
Warlord Champion, should the compound be crushed,
A pile of stones! (Indeed)
Great-Host-Slaying-Stranger! (True)
The day I come to know you, devouring of the knower.

Should we swear an oath,
Should we swear an oath, (Indeed)
The way the weak swear an oath,
And the manner of the mighty are
not the same. (That's the truth)
Village-Crusher and Village-Burier!
Hunter-Imposing-on-the-Hardy! (Indeed)
The league may lose, (Mmm)
But let them not become lovers of loss. (Mmm)
Simbon, Lion-Born-of-the-Cat! (Indeed)
I sing of the Stump-in-the-Dark-of-Night.
Should you bump against it,
It will bump against you.
The Granary-Guard-Dog, (Mmm)
It discerns not the stranger,
Nor discerns the familiar.
Should he come upon any person,
He will be bitten! (Mmm)
Kirikara Watita!
Adversity's-True-Place! (Indeed)
A man's reason and a woman's are not the same.
Pretty little words and truth are not the same.
No matter how long the road,
It always leads to someone's home. (That's true)

Ah! Bèmba! (Indeed)
Some old meddlers rose up;
"Ah! Du Kamisa, (Mmm)
"Being a woman is a malady! (Indeed)
"In my mind, (Indeed)
"You who with Leader-of-the-People
"Are of the same breast, (Indeed)
. . . (Indeed)
"And who come from the same belly, (Indeed)
"And who had a child, (Indeed)
"Who made a family sacrifice, (Indeed)
"Saying that you should be the outsider,
"And thus you should not eat of the meat.
"Being a woman is a malady!" (True)
At that, she became angry. (Indeed)
And went to find Magan Jata Kòndè of Du: (Indeed)
"Behold your lamb skin! (Mmm)

"I cannot be an outsider to you!
"I and your father are of the same cause,
"And suckled the same breast." (Mmm)
" . . . "
Magan Jata Kòndè of Du became enraged at that,
And seized his aunt, (Mmm)
And dragged her off, (Indeed)
And cast her in a hovel to the west of Du (Indeed)
And slashed off her breasts with a knife, magasi!
"You remain here! (Mmm)
"You have borne no children! (True)
"You remain here!
"You have borne no children! (True)

"My father was Leader-of-the-People.
"You have borne no children!" (Indeed)
"What? Did I not bear a child?" (Mmm)
"You have borne no children!"
"Come here!" (True)
She ripped off her calabash lid (Indeed)
And dipped her hand into the calabash:
"Do you not see your new-born hair?
"Did I not bear a child? (Indeed)
"Do you not see your navel cord?
"Did I not bear a child? (Indeed)
"The water breaking at your birth,
"The cloth on which it spilled,
"Behold that cloth before you!
"Alas! Did I not bear a child? (Indeed)
"Do you not see your swaddling cloth? (Indeed)
"Did I not bear a child?" (Indeed)
There is a proverb told in the Manden. (Indeed)
It is said of the Kòndès in the Manden. (Indeed)

To buy a boney horse. (Indeed)
To buy a boney horse. (Indeed)
If you deceive a man
To buy a boney horse,
You must deliver a grasscutter, too! (That's the truth,
There's no doubt)

The Kòndè matriarch grew furious. (Indeed)
The little old lady transformed herself,
And became a wild buffalo in the Manden. (Indeed)
Each of her horns: a golden spear and a silver spear. (Mmm)
Each of her ears: a golden snuff spoon, a silver snuff spoon. (Mmm)
The strands of her tail: needles of gold, needles of silver. (True)
Each of her ears: a golden snuff spoon, a silver snuff spoon. (Indeed)
Each of her hooves: an adze of gold, an adze of silver. (Indeed)
The woman thus transformed herself.
In the seven quarters of Du,
When the dawn would break,
She would slay a man in each quarter,
And thus they called her the Ginda of Du.
The Kòndè buffalo witch was called the Ginda of Du!

Ah! Bèmba! (Indeed)
Whenever two hunters went forth to fight the buffalo, (Indeed)
One would come back to tell the way the other died.
She would kill the one and leave the other (Mmm)
To go home and tell the way he died. (That's true)
The Taraweres heard about this matter. (Mmm)
  O Tura-Magan-and-Kanke-jan! (Indeed)
Dan Mansa Wulundin and Wulanba, (Indeed)
They took their bows and rose up. (Mmm)
What sitting will not solve,
Travel will resolve. (True)
They went forth. (Indeed)
They came to the deep forest. (Mmm)
In those days, kolas had not been created. (Indeed)
All the Manden fetishes were offered sacrifices of groundnuts.
A young jinn lived in one such fetish. (Indeed).
His name was Tinin Magan, the Pale. (Indeed)
Guinea-fowl feathers perforated the fetish.
  "Leprous-head-of-Gold, Tinin Magan, the Pale! (Indeed)

"Leprous-head-of-Silver, Tinin Magan, the Pale! (Indeed)
"Child of Nyagatè!
"Merchant Ben Magan without ostentation! (Indeed)
"The one who loves ostentation,
"Will he not make a merchant his friend? (Indeed)
"Gold is in the merchant's hand, (Indeed)
"That it may overflow on me, O Power! (Indeed)
"Silver is in the merchant's hand, (Indeed)
"That it may overflow on me, O Power!
"Going will I slay it? (Indeed)
"Coming will I slay it?"
As soon as he snapped the groundnut open,
He cast the shells. (Indeed)
One face up. (Indeed)
One face down. (True)

Ah, bards,
He who would cultivate,
Let him cultivate.
Son-Jara is done!
He who would deal in commerce,
Let him deal in commerce!
The Wizard is done! (Indeed)
These chords were played for him, my Father, in the Manden. (Mmm)
Son-Jara's tomb is in the Manden. (Indeed)
The village where his tomb is found, (Indeed)
The name of that village is Nyani, (True)
By the banks of the river, (Indeed)
On the banks of the Sankaran.
The name of the village is Nyani.
The Wizard's tomb is in Nyani. (Mmm)

Ah! Bèmba! (Indeed)
Dan Mansa Wulundin sat down. (Mmm)
He came and seized the jinn: (Indeed)
"My elder, come let us kill this jinn!"
"Ah! Little brother, do not kill the jinn.
"Leave him be, and he will read the signs for us.
"Jinns know more than the Sons-of-Adam." (Indeed)
And the jinn did conjury for them: (Indeed)

"When both of you go forth, (Mmm)
"You must seek sanctuary with the cordwainer patriarch,
"With Walali Ibrahima. (Indeed)
"When both of you go forth,
"You should sacrifice seven portions of goat, (Mmm)
"This and yesterday's leftover rice.
"There is an old woman to the west of Du.
"Give yesterday's rice to this old woman.
"And if God wills, you'll slay the buffalo." (Indeed)

They thus sought sanctuary with the cordwainer patriarch, (Indeed)
And sacrificed seven portions of goat. (Indeed)
Whenever they would go into the bush,
The buffalo would come into the town. (Mmm)
Whenever they would come into the town, (Indeed)
The buffalo would go into the bush.
They tracked each other for a week;
Not once did they and the buffalo meet. (True)

They sacrificed the leftover rice,
And offered it to the old woman.
She burst out laughing:
"Ha! And whose people are you?"
"We are Taraweres."
"Taraweres, what village do you hail from?" (Indeed)
"We hail from Bintanya Kamalen." (Indeed)
"Taraweres, I am the Buffalo of Du. (Indeed)
" 'Tis I brought an end to rice,
"And brought an end to fonio,
"And brought an end to groundnuts,
"And brought an end to people here, (Mmm)
"So none shall hear again the name of Kòndè! (Mmm)
" 'Tis I who am the Buffalo of Du.
"Taraweres, into your hands God has delivered me! (Indeed)

"Many eggs must you boil,
"And give to me, the old woman." (True)
They boiled up many eggs and put them together,
And gave them to the old woman.
She ate them down and drank her fill, (Indeed)

Till the folds of fat in her venter vanished. (Indeed)

"O Taraweres,
"Go forth and find two chicken eggs, (Indeed)
"These and a piece of green wood, (Indeed)
"This and a charcoal chunk, (Indeed)
"This and a spindle stick." (Indeed)
And she conjured a spell o'er all of that. (True)
"O Taraweres, let us swear an oath. (Indeed)
"Let Kòndè and Tarawere be bound by an oath."
They brought a new calabash bowl and turned it face down. (Indeed)
They linked their fingers each to the other: (Mmm)
"No friendship will be good!
"No love-making will be good! (Indeed)
"No brotherhood will be good!
"No marriage will be good!
"No love will be good,
"For any Tarawere son,
"Should a Kòndè he betray,
"Let that betrayal kill him! (Indeed)
"For any son of Kòndè, (Indeed)
"Should a Tarawere he betray,
"Let that betrayal kill him!" (Indeed)
Thus they swore the oath. (Indeed)
The Tarawere, they swore the oath (Indeed)
Over the black spitting cobra.
The Taraweres, they swore the oath (Indeed)
Over the crooked tooth mamba. (Indeed)
The Taraweres, they swore the oath
Over the dark black baobab. (Mmm)
The Kòndè woman, she swore the oath (Indeed)
Over the great deer fly
And the death-like stench of *datu*-leaf. (Mmm)
Whatever may remain, let that too be cast! (That's true)
O Tura-Magan-and-Kanke-jan! (True)

"Taraweres, when you go forth tomorrow, (Mmm)
"The buffalo which you may see, (Indeed)
"Each of her horns: a golden spear and a silver spear. (Indeed)

"The strands of her tail: needles of gold, needles of
silver. (Indeed)
"Each of her ears: a golden snuff spoon,
a silver snuff spoon. (Indeed)
"Each of her hooves: an adze of gold, an adze of silver.
"That is the Buffalo of Du. (True)

"Should she pursue you,
"You must throw down an egg.
"It will become a great wilderness. (Mmm)
"Before she traverses that wilderness, (Indeed)
"You must make some distance. (Mmm)
"When she pursues you again, (Indeed)
"You must throw down the other one.
"It will become a great lake. (Indeed)
"Plant the green stick at the edge of the lake. (Indeed)
"It will become a great forest. (Indeed)
"Behind the great forest will rise an anthill, (Indeed)
"Behind which should hide Dan Mansa Wulandin. (Indeed)
"Dan Mansa Wulanba (Mmm)
"Should climb into a tree. (Indeed)
"Dan Mansa Wulanba, (Indeed)
"On the charcoal chunk should step. (Indeed)
"Thus will he become a shade!" (Indeed)
Even tomorrow morning,
The Manden hunters will worship that Shadow.
That is what Shadow is! (True)

"Should you arm your bow with the spindle,
"And should you fire on the Buffalo of Du,
"I will leave this world behind.
"Taraweres, know this! I am the Buffalo of Du. (Mmm)
"No shot can pierce me. (Mmm)
"No spear can pierce me. (Mmm)
"No knife can pierce me. (Mmm)
"I brought an end to people,
"And brought an end to rice,
"And brought an end to fonio.
"O Taraweres!" (Mmm)

Ah! He who would cultivate,
Let him cultivate! (Mmm)
He who would deal in commerce,

Let him deal in commerce!
That was sung at the Wizard's tomb, my father,
At the Manden Sunkaran River,
On the banks of the Sankarandin.
The name of that village was Nyani.

The Taraweres took up the bow.
They reached the high bush country. (Mmm)
Dan Mansa Wulandin said, "O Elder,
"Behold the Buffalo of Du!" (Indeed)
The buffalo charged them, (Mmm)
And they threw down the first of the eggs. (Mmm)
It became a great wilderness.
There was a village in the midst of that wilderness.
The name of that village was Bèmbè.
Rescuer-King-of-the-Wilderness was there in the village of
Bèmbè.
Kamisòkò ancestor from Kiri,
Bee-King-of-the-Wilderness!
. . .
Tèrè Kumba and Kaya!
Nyani River and Maramu River!
But what grew beneath it apart from
hammer and bow? (Indeed. Eh,
(Fa-Digi, that's the truth)

Should you go north to Kaarta, (Mmm)
They call some of them there Magasa.
They are all of Fa-Koli's line.
Hero-of-Original-Clans.
. . . (True)

The buffalo charged them again,
And they threw down the other egg. (Mmm)
It became a great lake. (Indeed)
Dan Mansa Wulandin planted the green stick,
And it became a great forest. (Indeed)
Behind the forest was the anthill.
The buffalo went down to the lake.
She was swimming,
And she was drinking.
She was swimming,

And she was drinking.
Thus the bards sing of that: (Indeed)
The Kòndè lion child, Great-Water-Drinker! (Indeed)
Splasher-in-the-Lake! (Indeed)
Great-Lake-Water-Drinker! (Indeed)
Those-who-Turn, Fa-Kanda! (Indeed)
Those-who-Turn-About, Fa-Kanda! (Indeed)
Those-with-Visions, Fa-Kanda! (Indeed)
Those-who-Seek-Visions, Fa-Kanda! (Indeed)
Fa-Kanda, Killer-of-Kin!
Nineteen of them in all!
From these nineteen, Fa-Kanda gains power!
The arrow found in the breast of the brave, (Indeed)
It was Fa-Kanda's arrow. (Indeed)
The arrow found in the loins of the brave, (Indeed)
It was Fa-Kanda's arrow. (Indeed)
The arrow found in the brow of the brave, (Indeed)
It was Fa-Kanda's arrow.
Garabaya and Kaya! (Mmm)

Ah! Bèmba! (Indeed, I'm coming)
Biribiriba!
Kirikisa, Spear-of-Access, Spear-of-Service!
Nare Magan Kònatè!
Sorcerer-Seizing-Sorcerer! (Mmm)
Simbon, Lion-Born-of-the-Cat! (Mmm)

O Kala Jula Sangoyi Manunaka! (Indeed)
Dan Mansa Wulandin became deeply frightened: (Indeed)
"No spindle stick will ever pierce her hide!" (True)
He cleared the chamber of his gun,
And rammed some shot inside,
And discharged his powder on the buffalo. (Indeed)
The shot would not strike her. (Indeed)
She chased them on, biri-biri-biri!
They went and climbed a shea-butter tree. (Indeed)
The buffalo came up beneath them. (Indeed)
She shook her great head from side to side. (Indeed)
And bellowed out: (Indeed)
"Dense thicket! Shea tree's dense thicket!" (Indeed)

The shea tree branches with their people came crashing down to earth, biri! (Indeed)

And she pursued them once again, biri-biri-biri! (True)
Dan Mansa Wulanba climbed into another tree. (True)
Dan Mansa Wulandin
Went and hid behind the great anthill, (Indeed)
And stepped upon the charcoal chunk. (Indeed)
He said to his elder brother,
Said, "Let's do something now!"

The buffalo came round the anthill.
She looked both to and fro, (Indeed)
But nothing did she see.
She looked again both to and fro.
It was only Shadow in her sight,
That Shadow worshipped by the hunters. (Indeed)
She looked again both to and fro. (Indeed)
Dan Mansa Wulandin took the spindle stick,
Drew back and shot the Buffalo of Du, pan!
The buffalo bellowed out: "Oh!
  "O People of Du!
  "The Twisted Well! (Indeed)
  "Arrow-of-the-Knower!
  "Should your father be slain by the red buffalo,
  "And shall he see a red anthill,
  "Won't he be afraid of it?
  " 'Tis the Arrow-of-the-Knower!" (That's the truth)
And that has become a proverb. (Mmm, eh, Fa-Digi, that's the truth)

The buffalo collapsed, biri! (Indeed)
He hacked off her tail,
And hacked off her horns, (Indeed)
And hacked off her ears, (Indeed)
And hacked off her hooves. (Indeed)
Dan Mansa Wulanba came forward: (Indeed)
"Little brother, what has happened?" (Indeed)
"Ah, my elder," the reply, "the Buffalo of Du has fallen."
At which he cried out:
  "Snake country and fetish country!
  "Stench-of-Mosquito and Stench-of-Deerfly! (Indeed)
  "Cutter-of-Fresh-Heart and Cutter-of-Fresh-Liver!
  "King-of-the-Wilderness, Kininbi! (Mmm)
  "King-of-the-Wilderness, Kalinka!

"He-Who-Stands-within-the-Walls and He-Who-Stands-amongst-Great-Trees!
"For some the village is suitable,
"The outlands do not suit them.
"For some the outlands are suitable,
"The village does not suit them."
"Ah, my elder," the reply,
"Should you become a bard,
"One who could refuse you won't be found!" (That's the truth)
And from him thus descended Sangoyi, the Long Bow. (Indeed)
Sangoyi, the Long Bow, he begat Tuba Katè, (Indeed)
And begat Mònsòn Katè, (Indeed)
And begat Fatiyan Katè, (Indeed)
And begat Sagaburu Katè, the Tall, (Indeed)
And begat . . . (Indeed)
These are the six clans of Jebagatè bards. (That's true)

They each had two sons,
And thus became twelve in all.
One branch became the Kòròko. (True)
The Kòròko are bards. (Indeed, indeed)
Ah! Bèmba! (Indeed)
That Mònsòn Katè, (Indeed)
It was he who begat Bugu, the Bard. (Indeed)
Bugu, the Bard begat Bura Magasi. (Indeed)
Bura Magasi begat Madi, the Bard. (Indeed)
Madi, the Bard begat Tamba-keli Mansa Magan. (Indeed)
Mansa Magan begat Sigiya, (Indeed)
And Sigiya's son is this one right here. (Mmm, that's true)

O! Bèmba! (Indeed)
They brought the buffalo's horns and her hooves, (Indeed)
These and the strands of her tail. (Indeed)
They went and placed them all in a calabash. (Indeed)
Dan Mansa Wulandin drew his knife from its sheath,
And leaned it against the lounging platform. (Mmm)
Dan Mansa Wulanba, (Indeed)
He took his sandals off his feet, (Indeed)
And stacked them near the lounging platform, (Indeed)

And went to seek refuge with the cordwainer patriarch,
With Walali Ibrahima. (Indeed)

Old women and gossip are never far apart. (That's the truth)
A snuff-dipping little old woman came forward:
"Magan Jata Kòndè of Du, pass me a pinch of snuff." (Indeed)
He passed her a pinch of snuff. (Mmm)
She dipped some snuff and wet it down: (Indeed)
"I have a word to say to you.
"But let it remain between us two! (True)
"Say not you heard it from my lips! (Mmm)
"The buffalo that settled near our folk,
"Someone has slain that buffalo.
"And with that I'm off." (True)
Magan Jata Kòndè of Du let loose the great village drum. (Indeed)
He beat the royal drum, (Mmm)
The drum of power: (Mmm)
"Like it or not, (Mmm)
"Everyone must gather! (Indeed)
"The one who killed the buffalo, (True)
"Into two I have divided the twelve towns of Du,
"And to that person will give one half.
"Such a brave man will be an asset to our folk."
No need to kill for the leper,
But one footstep forward, (Indeed)
That is all he wants.

Ah, he who would cultivate,
Let him cultivate.
Ah! Bards, he who would deal in commerce,
Let him deal in commerce!
Son-Jara is done!

O Nare Magan Kònatè!
From Fatiyataligara
All the way to Sokoto, (Indeed)
All that was Magan Son-Jara's,
The Africans call that, my father,
The Republic of Mali, (Indeed)

The Maninka realm, (Mmm)
That is the meaning of Mali.
He slayed Bambara-of-the-Border. (Indeed)
Settling on the border does not suit the weak. (Indeed)
And killed Bambara-the-Lizard, (Indeed)
No weak one should call himself Lizard, (Indeed)
And slayed Bambara-of-the-Backwoods, (Indeed)
Settling the backwoods does not suit the weak. (True)
I sing this for Modibo, (Mmm)
Daba's Modibo! (Indeed)
Modibo descended from Lamuru.
Modibo who was fathered by Daba.
That Daba, he was fathered by Lamuru in
Bukunun Jirè. (Indeed)
A Kamara woman was Modibo's mother.
But Son-Jara did not have the wind as shoes,
To travel far and wide upon. (Indeed)
But that was done by Modibo.
O Nare Magan Kònatè!
The Sorcerer-Seizing-Sorcerer! (Indeed)

Ah! Bèmba! (True)
Some strong young braves came forward,
And wiped off the blade of the knife. (Indeed)
Whoever would put the blade in his sheath,
If it wasn't too big, it was too small. (Indeed)
Others came forward, (Indeed)
And put their feet into the sandals.
If they weren't too big, they were too small. (Mmm)

They sent a messenger to the cordwainer patriarch,
To Walali Ibrahima, (Mmm)
To Ibrahima.
Dan Mansa Wulandin and Wulanba went to the
meeting. (Indeed)
Tura Magan came forward!
The Taraweres came forward! (Indeed)
They arrived at the compound door,
By the rubbish heap. (Indeed)
An old male dog sidled up (Indeed)
With a cat beside him. (True)

The old dog spoke out: (True)
"Ah! Taraweres! (Indeed)
"I thank you for the rice. (Indeed)
"I thank you for those bits of bone.
"Be kind to people.
"If one is kind to people,
"Should there be no recompense,
"At least it will be known of him. (That's true)

"Taraweres, you are off to this meeting. (Indeed)
"When the twelve towns of Du are divided in two,
"And the half offered unto you,
"So that you'll settle here, (Indeed)
"You must refuse! (Indeed)
"You must say, 'We come from the Manden, (Indeed)
" 'We return to the Manden.'
"O Taraweres! (True)

"There will be six young maidens there. (Mmm)
"When you are told to choose amongst them, (Indeed)
"This black cat will I release,
"So that she will approach you. (True)
"The maiden's legs she goes between, (Indeed)
"Comes out, goes round and through again, (Indeed)
"And goes again between her legs, (Indeed)
"Comes out, goes round and through again, (Indeed)
"That is the maiden you must take. (Indeed)
"Her name will be Sugulun Kòndè. (Indeed)
"Warts and pustules cover her. (Indeed)
"They call her Sugulun-of-the-Warts! (Indeed)
"Should you go forth with her, (Indeed)
"Her only son once born, (Indeed)
"The Manden will be his. (Indeed)
"O Taraweres, I thank you!" (Indeed)

On that, Dan Mansa Wuladin went forth (Indeed)
And slipped the knife into its sheath,
And sat down on the lounging platform. (Indeed)
Dan Mansa Wulanba, (Indeed)
He slipped his feet into the sandals, (Indeed)

And sat down upon the lounging platform. (Indeed)

All cried out: " 'Tis they who killed the buffalo! (Indeed)
" 'Tis they who killed the buffalo! (Mmm)
"Whose people are you?"
"We are the Taraweres." (True)
"And where do you hail from?" (Mmm)
"We come from Bintanya Kamalen." (Indeed)
"O Taraweres! (Mmm)
"The twelve towns of Du, I'll divide in twain,
"And give one half to you, (Mmm)
"So that you'll settle here. (Mmm)
"Such brave men complement the village folk." (True)
"That cannot be us!
"We come from the Manden.
"And to the Manden we'll return."
"Taraweres, look about you then. (True)
"Whatever maiden you may see
"Will be your struggle's reward.
"Whichever woman you may see,
" 'Tis her that I will give to you." (True)
They brought the maidens forward, (True)
Six young maidens. (Mmm)
The one behind whom the Kòndè girl stood, (Indeed)
She cried out, saying, "Get from behind me! (Indeed)
"Let me not with you be made so vile!" (That's true)
They all moved away and stood apart. (Mmm)

The black cat moved upon the ground.
It turned around and round.
It turned around and round. (Indeed)
It passed between the Kòndè Maiden's legs,
Came out, turned round, and through again. (Indeed)
The Taraweres came running up
And seized the Kòndè Maiden by the right hand.
"Behold our maiden! (Indeed)
"Behold our maiden!
"We have seen our maiden!"

At that time, the sacred knife
Of the Tarawere ancestor

Was in the hands of Tura-Magan-and-Kanke-jan.
When he drew it from its sheath, (Indeed)
When his eyes fell upon the blade, (Indeed)
He could not put it back again
Were no man's blood upon it. (Indeed)

Were he to unsheath the sacred knife, (Indeed)
And having grasped it, lick it, (Indeed)
Were he to lay it on a wart,
That wart would fade away. (True)

When now he drew the sacred knife, (Indeed)
And having grasped it, licked it, (Indeed)
And when he laid it on the Kòndè maiden's sores,
Those leprous sores did fade away. (True)

All her leprous sores did fade away. (Indeed)
"So, Kòndès, we have found our maiden.
"We must be on our way! (Indeed)
"What sitting will not solve,
"Travel will resolve. (True)
"We must be on our way!" (True)

EPISODE FOUR: THE MANDEN

And thus they rose and journeyed forth (Mmm)
From the time the sun rose (Indeed)
Until the sun fell. (Indeed)
As they reached a certain village, (Indeed)
Dan Mansa Wulandin said, "My elder, (Indeed)
"Should the elder and the younger venture forth,
"To seek their fortune together, (Indeed)
"Should it be wealth they find, (Indeed)
"They should use it to marry a wife,
"Giving her to the elder. (Indeed)
"Whatever may be found after that, (Indeed)
"Should be given to the younger. (Indeed)
"This woman then should stay with you.
"Whatever may be found next time,
"Let that maiden be mine!" (Mmm)

They entered the town. (Indeed)
Dan Mansa Wulanba (Indeed)
With the maiden entered a hut. (True)
The night had passed its prime, lelelele! (Mmm)
Dan Mansa Wulandin lay down outside. (Indeed)
Dan Mansa Wulanba rose up, (True)
To seek pleasure and duty with his wife. (Indeed)
He laid his hand on the Kòndè maid. (Indeed)
Now, all women were taller than Sugulun Kòndè.
All of them larger than Sugulun Kòndè.
But she stretched out: bilililili,
Putting her feet against the back wall, (Mmm)
And laying her head at the door,
And projected two spikes from her breasts. (Indeed)

"O Tarawere! Lie back down! (Indeed)
"My husband's in the Manden.
"And your wife will be there, too!" (True)
Dan Mansa Wulanba came running outside:
"Ha! Hey!"
Dan Mansa Wulandin said:
"My brother, what has happened?"
"Ah, little brother!
"All women are taller than Sugulun Kòndè;
"All of them larger than Sugulun Kòndè;
"Yet when I put my hand on her, (Indeed)
"Saying I sought pleasure and duty with my wife,
"She stretched herself: bilililili,
"Putting her feet against the back wall, (Mmm)
"And laying her head at the door,
"And projecting two spikes from her breasts,
"And told me to lie back down, (Mmm)
"Saying that her husband's in the Manden,
"And that my wife would be there, too."
They both lay back down (Indeed)
Until the break of day. (Mmm)
At that they rose up. (Indeed)
Now, Fata Magan, the Handsome was about to leave that town.
He was leaving to trade in a far market. (Mmm)
But a jinn came and laid a hand on him: (Mmm)
"Stay right here! (Indeed)

"Two youths have come amongst us, (Mmm)
"Two youths with an ugly young maid. (Mmm)
"Should you come by that ugly maid, (Mmm)
"She will bear you a son. (Indeed)
"The Manden will belong to him." (Indeed)

O! Bèmba! (Indeed)
I sing of the Sorcerer's future; (Mmm, that's true)
Of the life ahead of Son-Jara!
There were two ways to greet in the Manden of Old. (Mmm)
Brave young men said, "Ilu tuntun!" (That's true)
To which the reply, "Tuntun bèrè!"
The women said, "Ilu kònkòn!"
To which the reply, "Kònkòn lògòsò!" (Indeed)
The Taraweres came forward: (True)
"I tuntun!"
He answered them, "Tuntun bèrè! (Mmm)
"Where do you come from?
"Where are you going?"
"We have come from the land of Du.
"We go to Bintanya Kamalen."
"Whose people are you?" (Mmm)
"We are Taraweres." (Mmm)
"O Taraweres,
"Were this young prince to find the right wife, (Mmm)
"She would be the reward of a Tarawere struggle. (True)

"My flesh-and-blood sister is here, (Indeed)
"Nakana Tiliba. (Indeed)
"I will give her to you.
"You must give me your ugly maid. (Mmm)
"My forefather Bilal, (Indeed)
"When he departed from the Messenger of God, (True)
"He designed a certain token, (Mmm)
"Saying that his ninth descendant, (Indeed)
"Having taken his first wife, (True)
"When he takes his second wife, (Indeed)
"Must add that token to that marriage. (Mmm)
"I am adding that token
"Together with Nakana Tiliba, (Mmm)
"And giving them to you,

"You must give me your ugly little maid."
That token was added to Nakana Tiliba,
Exchanging her for Sugulun Kòndè. (Indeed)
It is said that Fata Magan, the Handsome
Took the Kòndè maiden to bed. (Mmm)
His Berete wife became pregnant. (Indeed)
His Kòndè wife became pregnant. (Indeed)

One day as dawn was breaking, (Indeed)
The Berete woman gave birth to a son. (Indeed)
She cried out, "Ha! Old Women! (Indeed)
"That which causes co-wife conflict
"Is nothing but the co-wife's child. (True)
"Go forth and tell my husband (Indeed)
"His first wife has borne him a son." (Indeed)

The old women came up running. (Indeed)
"Alu kònkòn!" (Mmm)
They replied to them, "Kònkòn dògòsò!
"Come let us eat." (Mmm)
They fixed their eyes on one another:
"Ah! Man must swallow his saliva!" (True)
They sat down around the food. (Indeed)
The Kòndè woman then bore a son. (Indeed)
They sent the Kuyatè matriarch, Tumu Maniya: (Indeed)
"Tumu Maniya, go tell it, (True)
"Tell Fata Magan, the Handsome,
"Say, 'the Tarawere trip to Du was good.' (True)
"Say, 'the ugly maid they brought with them,'
"Say, 'that woman has just borne a son.' " (True)

The Kuyatè matriarch came forward: (True)
"Alu kònkòn!" (Mmm)
They replied to her, "Kònkòn dògòsò! (Indeed)
"Come and let us eat."

[The female bard Tumu Maniya goes to find the king and, like the old women who preceded her, is also invited to eat, but she rejects the food until her message is delivered. The announcing of the birth of Son-Jara first, though he was actually born second, causes the father to designate him as first-born. The old women then burst out their message of the Berete woman's child, but alas, they are too late. The reversal of announcements is viewed as theft of birthright (see note for line 1 concerning Son-Jara's surname Keyta), and the Berete woman is understandably furious at the old women, who flop their hands about nervously.]

Some just flopped their hands about:
"I will not hear of this from anyone!
"I spent a sleepless night.
"The lids of my eyes are dried out,
bèrè-bèrè-bèrè. (That's true)
"But I will not hear of this from anyone!"
Some just clasped their hands together.
What travail it had become!
Ha! The old woman had forgotten her message
And abandoned it for a meal.
Those-Caught-by-their-Craws!
That was the first day of battle in the Manden.
Pandemonium broke loose! bòkòlen!

I sing of Biribiriba.
Ah! He who would cultivate,
Let him cultivate. (Mmm)
He who would deal in commerce,
Let him deal in commerce! (That's true)

Ah! Bèmba! (Mmm)
War may give to some, my father,
Although it be not theirs.
War may take from some,
Although it be their own.
If there be no war,
Men of power would not be known. (Indeed)

Both women were confined in one hut.
Pandemonium broke loose! bòkòlen! (Indeed)
Saman Berete,
The daughter of Tall Magan Berete-of-the-Ruins,
Saman Berete, (Indeed)
Still bloodstained, she came out. (Indeed)
"What happened then?
"O Messengers, what happened? (Indeed)

"O Messengers, what became of the message?" (Indeed)

The Kuyatè matriarch spoke out:
"Nothing happened at all. (Indeed)
"I was the first to pronounce myself. (Indeed)
"Your husband said the first name heard,
"Said, he would be the elder, (Indeed)
"And thus yours became the younger." (Indeed)
She cried out, "Old women, (Indeed)
"Now you have really reached the limit! (True)
"I was the first to marry my husband,
"And the first to bear him a son. (Indeed)
"Now you have made him the younger. (Indeed)
"You have really reached your limit!"
She spoke then to her younger co-wife, (Indeed)
"Oh Lucky Karunga, (Indeed)
"For you marriage has turned sweet. (Indeed)
"A first son birth is the work of old,
"And yours has become the elder." (That's the truth)

The infants were bathed. (Indeed)
Both were laid beneath a cloth. (Indeed)
The grandmother had gone to fetch firewood. (Indeed)
The old mother had gone to fe . . . , to fetch firewood. (Indeed)
She then quit the firewood-fetching place,
And came and left her load of wood. (Indeed)
She came into the hut. (Indeed)
She cast her eye on the Berete woman, (Indeed)
And cast her eye on the Kòndè woman, (Indeed)
And looked the Berete woman over,
And looked the Kòndè woman over. (Indeed)

She lifted the edge of the cloth.
And examined the child of the Berete woman,
And lifted again the edge of the cloth,
And examined the child of the Kòndè woman. (Indeed)
From the very top of Son-Jara's head, (Indeed)
To the very tip of his toes, all hair! (Indeed)

The old mother went outside. (Indeed)
She laughed out: "Ha! Birth-givers! Hurrah!

"The little mother has borne a lion thief." (That's true)
Thus gave the old mother Son-Jara his name. (Indeed)
"Givers of birth, Hurrah!
"The little mother has borne a lion thief. (That's true)
"Hurrah! The mother has given birth to a lion thief."
Biribiriba! (Indeed)
And thus they say of him,
Son-Jara, Nare Magan Kònatè. (Indeed)
Simbon, Lion-Born-of-the-Cat. (Indeed)
The Berete woman,
She summoned to her a holy-man,
Charging him to pray to God, (Indeed)
So Son-Jara would not walk. (Indeed)
And summoned to her an Omen Master, (Indeed)
For him to read the signs in sand, (Indeed)
So Son-Jara would not walk. (Indeed)

For nine years, Son-Jara crawled upon the ground. (Indeed)
Magan Kònatè could not rise. (Indeed)
The benefactor of the Kòndè woman's child,
It was a jinn Magan Son-Jara had. (Indeed)
His name was Tanimunari.
Tanimunari, (Indeed)
He took the lame Son-Jara (Indeed)
And made the ḥājj (Indeed)
To the gates of the Kaabah. (Indeed)
Have you never heard this warrant of his ḥājj? (Indeed)
"Ah! God! (Indeed)
"I am the man for the morrow. (Indeed)
"I am the man for the day to follow. (Indeed)
"I will rule over the bards, (Indeed)
"And the three and thirty warrior clans.
"I will rule over all these people. (Indeed)
"The Manden shall be mine!" (Indeed)
That is how he made the ḥājj.
He took him up still lame,
And brought him back to Bintanya Kamalen. (Indeed)
In the month before Dònba, (Indeed)
On the twenty-fifth day,
The Berete woman's Omen Master emerged from retreat: (Indeed)
"Damn! My fingers are worn out! (Indeed)
"My buttocks are worn out! (Indeed)

"A tragic thing will come to pass in the Manden. (Indeed)
"There is no remedy to stop it.
"There is no sacrifice to halt it.
"Its cause cannot be ascertained, (Indeed)
"Until two rams be sacrificed. (Indeed)

"The one for Son-Jara, a black-headed ram. (True)
"Dankaran Tuma, an all white ram. (Indeed)
"Have them do battle this very day." (Indeed)
By the time of the midday meal,
Son-Jara's ram had won. (Indeed)
They slaughtered both the rams, (Indeed)
And cast them down a well,
So the deed would not be known. (Indeed)
But known it did become. (Indeed)
  Knowing never fails its time,
  Except its day not come. (That's true, eh, Fa-Digi, that's true)

In the month before Dònba (That's true)
On the twenty-seventh day, (Indeed)
The holy-man emerged from his retreat! (Indeed)
"Hey! A tragic thing will come to pass in the Manden. (Indeed)
"There is no remedy to stop it.
"There is no sacrifice to halt it. (Indeed)
"Its cause cannot be ascertained,
"Until a toothless dog be sacrificed."
Now whoever saw a toothless dog in the Manden? (Indeed)
They went forth to Kong, (Indeed)
And bought a snub-nosed dog, (Indeed)
A little spotted dog,
And pulled its teeth with pliers,
And mixed a potion for its mouth, (Indeed)
And brought it back to the Manden,
Saying, with this toothless dog, (Indeed)
Saying, Magan Kònatè should not walk. (Indeed)
Son-Jara should not rise!
  Ah! Bards, he who would cultivate,
  Let him cultivate!
  Ah, he who would deal in commerce,
  Let him deal in commerce!
  From Fatiyataligara, (Indeed)

All the way to Sokoto, (Indeed)
All that was Magan Son-Jara's, (Indeed)
The Africans call that, my father,
The Republic of Mali, (Indeed)
The Maninka realm. (Indeed)
He slayed Bambara-of-the-Border; (Indeed)
Settling on the border does not suit the weak, (Indeed)
And slayed Bambara-the-Lizard; (Indeed)
No weak one should call himself lizard, (Indeed)
And slayed Bambara-of-the-Backwoods; (Indeed)
Settling the backwoods does not suit the weak, (True)
But he did not make airplanes his shoes
For to travel far and wide. (Indeed)
The one to do that was Modibo, (Indeed)
Daba's Modibo, (Mmm)
The President of the Republic, (Indeed)
The Kamara woman's child, beloved one,
It was he! (The Kamara woman . . . , that's the truth)

Biribiriba, Nare Magan Kònatè! (Indeed)
The bards sing of you, my father,
The Sorcerer-Seizing-Sorcerer!
A man of power is hard to find. (And how about what you did in Dakar?)

But I have laid my hand on Daba's Modibo, (Indeed)
Modibo who was fathered by Daba. (Indeed)
That Daba was fathered by Lamuru in Bakunun Jire. (Indeed)
Fatuma Kamara, Disperser-of-Women!
O! Modibo! (Indeed)
The Kamara woman's lion-man!
O! Modibo!
O Nare Magan Kònatè! (Mmm, that's true)

Ah! Bèmba! (Indeed)
They made a sacrifice of the spotted dog (Indeed)
So that the Wizard would not walk. (Indeed)
In the month of Dòmba, (Indeed)
The very, very, very first day, (Indeed)
Son-Jara's Muslim jinn came forward: (Indeed)
"That which God has said to me, (Indeed)
"To me Tanimunari, (Indeed)

"That which God has said to me, (Indeed)
"So it will be done. (Indeed)
"When the month of Dòmba is ten days old, (Indeed)
"Son-Jara will rise and walk." (Indeed)
In the month of Dòmba, (Indeed)
On its twelfth day, (Indeed)
The Messenger of God was born. (Indeed)
On the thirteenth day, (Indeed)
Jòn Bilal was born. (Indeed)
On its tenth day, (Indeed)
Was the day for Son-Jara to walk.

O Nare Magan Kònatè! (That's true)
. . .
Master and Warrior Master!
O Nare Magan Kònatè!
O Sorcerer-Seizing-Sorcerer!
A man of power is hard to find. (Mmm)
All people with their empty words,
They all seek to be men of power. (That's true)
Ministers, deputies and presidents, (Indeed)
All of them seek after power,
But there is no easy way to power. (That's true)

Here in our Mali,
We have found our freedom. (Indeed)
Though a person find no gold,
Though he find no silver, (Indeed)
Should he find his freedom,
Then noble will he be. (That's the truth)
A man of power is hard to find. (Mmm)
Ah! Bèmba!

On the tenth day of Dòmba, (Indeed)
The Wizard's mother cooked some couscous, (Indeed)
Sacrificial couscous for Son-Jara.
Whatever woman's door she went to, (Indeed)
The Wizard's mother would cry: (Indeed)
"Give me some sauce of baobab leaf." (Indeed)
The woman would retort,
"I have some sauce of baobab leaf,
"But it is not to give to you.
"Go tell that cripple child of yours

"That he should harvest some for you. (Mmm)
" 'Twas my son harvested these for me." (True)

And bitterly did she weep: bilika bilika.
She went to another woman's door; (Mmm)
That one too did say: (Mmm)
"I have some sauce of baobab leaf,
"But it is not to give to you.
"Go tell that cripple child of yours
"That he should harvest some for you.
" 'Twas my son harvested these for me." (True)

With bitter tears, the Kòndè woman
came back, bilika bilika.
"King of Nyani, King of Nyani,
"Will you never rise? (Mmm)
"King of Nyani, King of Nyani,
"Will you never rise? (Mmm)
"King of Nyani with helm of mail,
"He says he fears no man.
"Will you never rise?
"Rise up, O King of Nyani! (That's true)

"King of Nyani, King of Nyani,
"Will you never rise?
"King of Nyani with shirt of mail,
"He says he fears no man.
"Will you never rise?
"Rise up, O King of Nyani! (True)

"O Wizard, I have failed!" (True)
"Ah, my mother,
"There is a thickener, I hear, called black *lele*. (True)
"Why not put some in my sauce?
"'Tis the thickener grown in gravel."

She put black *lele* in the couscous.
The Wizard ate of it.
Ma'an Kònatè ate his fill: (True)
"My mother, (Indeed)
"Go to the home of the blacksmith patriarchs, (Indeed)
"To Dun Fayiri and Nun Fayiri. (Indeed)
"Have them shape a staff, seven-fold forged,
"So that Magan Kònatè may rise up." (Indeed)

The blacksmith patriarchs shaped a staff, seven-fold
forged. (Indeed)
The Wizard came forward. (Indeed)
He put his right hand o'er his left,
And upwards drew himself, (Indeed)
And upwards drew himself.
He had but reached the halfway point. (Indeed)
"Take this staff away from me!"
Magan Kònatè did not rise. (True)

In misery his mother wept: bilika bilika: (Indeed)
"Giving birth has made me suffer!" (Mmm)
"Ah, my mother, (Mmm)
"Return to the blacksmith patriarchs. (Indeed)
"Ask that they forge that staff anew, (Indeed)
"And shape it twice again in size. (Mmm)
"Today I arise, my holy-man said." (Mmm)

The patriarchs of the smiths forged the staff,
Shaping it twice again in size. (True)
They forged that staff,
And gave it to Ma'an Kònatè. (Indeed)
He put his right hand o'er his left, (Indeed)
And upwards Son-Jara drew himself. (Indeed)
Upwards Nare Magan Kònatè drew himself. (Indeed)

Again he reached the halfway point: (Mmm)
"Take this staff away from me!"
Ma'an Kònatè did not rise.
He sat back down again. (Indeed)
His mother wrung her hands atop her head,
And wailed: "dèndèlen!
"Giving birth has made me suffer!" (True)
"Ah, my mother, (Mmm)
"Whate'er has come twixt you and God, (Indeed)
"Go and speak to God about it now!" (Indeed)

On that, his mother left,
And went to the east of Bintanya, (Indeed)
To seek a custard apple tree. (Indeed)

Ah! Bèmba! (Indeed)
And found some custard apple trees, (Indeed)
And cut one down, (Indeed)

And trimmed it level to her breast, (Indeed)
And stood as if in prayer: (Indeed)
"O God!
"For Son-Jara I have made this staff. (Indeed)
"If he be the man for the morrow, (Indeed)
"If he be the man for the day to follow, (Indeed)
"If he is to rule the bards, (Indeed)
"If he is to rule the smiths, (Indeed)
"The three and thirty warrior clans, (Indeed)
"If he is to rule all those, (Indeed)
"When this staff I give to Nare Magan Kònatè, (Indeed)
"Let Magan Kònatè arise. (True)
"If he be not the man for the morrow, (Indeed)
"If he be not the man for the day to follow, (Indeed)
"If he is not to rule the bards, (Indeed)
"If he is not to rule the smiths, (Indeed)
"When this staff I give to the King of Nyani,
"Let Son-Jara not arise.
"O God, from the day of my creation, (Indeed)
"If I have known another man,
"Save Fata Magan, the Handsome alone,
"When this staff I give to the King of Nyani,
"Let Son-Jara arise. (Indeed)
"From the day of my creation, (True)
"If I have known a second man,
"And not just Fata Magan, the Handsome, (Indeed)
"Let Ma'an Kònatè not arise!" (True)

She cut down that staff,
Going to give it to Nare Magan Kònatè,
To the Kòndè woman's child, the Answerer-of-Needs! (True)
The Wizard took the staff, (Mmm)
And put his right hand o'er his left, (Indeed)
And upwards drew himself, (Indeed)
And upwards drew himself.
Magan Kònatè rose up! (Mmm)
Running, his mother came forward,
And clasped his legs
And squeezed them, (Indeed)
And squeezed them: (True)
"This home of ours,
"The home of happiness. (Indeed)

"Happiness did not pass us by.
"Magan Kònatè has risen!" (Indeed)
"Oh! Today! (Indeed)
"Today is sweet! (Indeed)
"God the King ne'er made today's equal! (Indeed)
"Ma'an Kònatè has risen!" (Indeed)
"There is no way of standing without worth.
"Behold his way of standing: danka!
"O Kapok Tree and Flame Tree!" (Fa-Digi, that's true)
"My mother, (Mmm)
"That baobab there in Manden country,
"That baobab from which the best sauce comes, (Indeed)
"Where is that baobab, my mother?" (Indeed)
"Ah, my lame one, (Indeed)
"You have yet to walk." (Indeed)

The Wizard took his right foot,
And put it before his left. (Indeed)
His mother followed behind him,
And sang these songs for him: (Indeed)
"Tunyu Tanya! (Indeed)
"Brave men fit well among warriors! (Indeed)
"Tunyu tanya! (Indeed)
"Brave men fit well among warriors! (Indeed)
"Ma'an Kònatè, you have risen!" (Indeed)

"Muddy water, (Indeed)
"Do not compare yourself to water among the stones. (Indeed)
"That among the stones is pure, wasili! (Indeed)
" . . . (Indeed)
" . . . (Indeed)
"And a good reputation. (Indeed)
"Khalif Magan Kònatè has risen. (True)

"Great snake, O great snake, (Indeed)
"I will tolerate you. (Indeed)
"Should you confront me, toleration. (Indeed)
"O great snake upon the path, (Indeed)
"Whatever confronts me, I will tolerate." (Indeed)

"Arrow-shaft of happiness. (Indeed)
"It is in one hundred. (Indeed)
"The one hundred dead,
"All but Son-Jara. (True)

"The higher stones get crushed! (Indeed)
"Who can mistake the Destroyer-of-Origins!
"And this by the hand of Nare Magan Kònatè!"

Hey! Biribiriba came forward. (Indeed)
He shook the baobab tree. (Indeed)
A young boy fell out.
His leg was broken.
The bards thus sing, "Leg-Crushing-Ruler!
"Magan Kònatè has risen!" (Indeed)
He shook the baobab again. (Indeed)
Another young boy fell out.
His arm was broken (Indeed)
The bards thus sing, "Arm-Breaking-Ruler!
"Magan Kònatè has risen!" (Indeed)
He shook the baobab again. (Indeed)
Another young boy fell out. (Indeed)
His neck was broken. (Indeed)
And thus the bards sing, "Neck-Breaking-Ruler!
"Magan Kònatè has risen!" (Indeed)
The Wizard uprooted the baobab tree,
And laid it across his shoulder. (Mmm)
Nare Magan Kònatè rose up. (Indeed)

A crowd of women surged out: yrrrrrrr. (Indeed)
"Why have you come today? (Indeed)
"What a spectacle! (Indeed)
"Have they no reason to be here? (Indeed)
"What a spectacle!" (Indeed)

"O witch-wives! (Indeed)
"O witch-wives of the Manden!
"You go find the answer. (Indeed)
"Today's cannot be found by searching." (Indeed)

"The Master of men, O power, power, power. (Indeed)
"One without people, the wind, the wind.
"The woman put the child in a web, (?)
"A web of sorcery!" (?) (Mmm)

They fixed their eyes on Magan Son-Jara standing there:
"Come, let us go!
"Nare Magan Kònatè has risen!

"Living alone, I know it. (Indeed)
"After coming to understand that, (Indeed)
"Bearer of good children, have no shame. (Indeed)
"Whenever there's a crowd, have no shame."

"Having power, (Indeed)
"If you prepare yourself for the powerful,
"They will respect you." (Indeed)

"The pocket sees only today,
"Its eye is not on tomorrow. (Indeed)
"The pocket sees only today, (Indeed)
"Its eye is not on tomorrow.
"A fortunate man's happiness occurs while he lives. (?) (Indeed)
"The unfortunate man's happiness occurs after he dies.
"O misery! (Indeed)
"But one should not kill himself for misery.
"No one knows where misery leads. (True)
"Khalif Magan Kònatè!

"The one for those behind is Kapok.
"Tunyu tanya! (Indeed)
"Ours is the Flame Tree,
"The golden Flame Tree! (Mmm)
"Khalif Magan Kònatè has risen!"

Biribiriba came forward. (Mmm)
He planted the baobab behind his mother's house:
"In and about the Manden, (Mmm)
"From my mother they must seek these leaves!" (Mmm)
To which his mother said, "I do not think I heard." (Mmm)
"Ah, my mother, (Indeed)
"Now all the Manden baobabs are yours."
"I do not think I heard."
"Ah, my mother, (Indeed)
"All those women who refused you leaves,
"They all must seek those leaves from you." (Indeed)
His mother fell upon her knees, gɛjebu!
On both her knees,
And laid her head aside the baobab. (Indeed)

"For years and years,
"My ear was deaf. (Indeed)
"Only this year
"Has my ear heard news.
"Khalif Magan Kònatè has risen!" (That's true)
Biribiriba! (Indeed)
Since he began to walk, (Indeed)
Whenever he went into the bush, (Mmm)
Were he to kill some game, (Indeed)
He would give his elder the tail,
And think no more of it.
. . . (Indeed)

Took up the bow!
Simbon, Master-of-the-Bush!
Took up the bow!
Took up the bow! (Indeed)
Ruler of bards and smiths
Took up the bow!
Took up the bow!
The Kòndè woman's child,
Answerer-of-Needs,
He took up the bow.
Sugulun's Ma'an took up the bow!

The Wizard has risen!
King of Nyani, Nare Magan Kònatè!
The Wizard has risen! (Indeed)
Ah! Bèmba! (Indeed)
Whenever he went to the bush, (Indeed)
Were he to kill some game, (Indeed)
He would give to his elder the tail,
And think no more of it.
. . . (Indeed)
As Biribiriba walked forth one day, (That's true)
A jinn came upon him,
And laid his hand on Son-Jara's shoulder:
"O Son-Jara! (Mmm)
"In the Manden, there's a plot against you. (Mmm)
"That spotted dog you see before you, (Indeed)
"Is an offering made against you, (Indeed)
"So that you not rule the bards, (Indeed)

"So that you not rule the smiths,
"So, the three and thirty warrior clans,
"That you rule over none of them. (Mmm)
"When you go forth today, (Mmm)
"Make an offering of a safo-dog, (Indeed)
"Should God will it,
"The Manden will be yours!" (Indeed)

Ah! Bèmba!
On that, Biribiriba went forth, my father,
And made an offering of a safo-dog,
And hung a weight around its neck,
And fastened an iron chain about it. (Indeed)
Even tomorrow morning,
The Europeans will imitate him.
Whenever the Europeans leave a dog, (Mmm)
Its neck weight,
They fasten that dog with an iron chain, Manden! (Indeed)

O! Bèmba!
He hung a weight around the dog's neck,
And fastened it with a chain. (Mmm)
That done, whatever home he passed before, (Indeed)
The people stood gaping at him:
"Causer-of-Loss! (Indeed)
"A cow with its neckweight,
"But a dog with a neckweight?" (Indeed)
To which the Wizard did retort:
"Leave me be! (True)
"Cast your eyes on the dog of the prince.
"There's not a tooth in that dog's mouth!
"But there are teeth in my dog's mouth,
"My commoner's dog. Leave me be! (Indeed)
"My dog's name is Tomorrow's Affair."

Son-Jara's sacrificial dog,
That dog was called Tomorrow's Affair.

From his neckweight he broke loose,
And also from his chain, (Indeed)
And charged the dog of Dankaran Tuman, (Indeed)

And ripped him into shreds, fèsè fèsè fèsè! (Indeed)
And stacked one piece atop the other. (Indeed)
The mother of Dankaran Tuman, she wrung her hands atop her head,
And gave a piercing cry: "dèndèlen! (Indeed)
"That a dog would bite a dog, (Indeed)
"A natural thing in the Manden. (Indeed)
"That a dog would kill a dog,
"A natural thing in the Manden.
"That a dog shred another like an old cloth,
"My mother, there must be something with his master!"
Dankaran Tuman replied, "Ah! my mother, (Mmm)
"I called my dog Younger-Leave-Me-Be. (Mmm)
"Ah! My mother, do not sever the bonds of family. (True)
"My mother! (Indeed)
"That is the dog that stalked the bush
"To go and kill some game,
"Bringing it back to me, my mother. (True)
"Do not sever the bonds of family, my mother!" (True)

The mother of Dankaran Tuman had no answer: (Indeed)
"One afternoon, the time will come for Son-Jara to depart. (Mmm)
"Indeed what the wise men have said, (Mmm)
"His time is for the morrow. (Mmm)
"The one that I have borne, (Mmm)
"He is being left behind without explanation. (Mmm)
"Son-Jara, (Mmm)
"The Kòndè woman's offspring, (Mmm)
"He will take the Manden tribute, (Mmm)
"And he will rule the bards, (Mmm)
"And he will rule the smiths, (Indeed)
"And rule the funès and the cordwainers. (Indeed)
"The Manden will be his.
"That time will yet arrive, (Indeed)
"And that by the hand of Nare Magan Kònatè.
"Nothing leaves its time behind."
O Biribiriba!
Kirikisa, Spear-of-Access, Spear-of-Service!
People of Kaya, Son-Jara entered Kaya.
All this by the hand of Nare Magan Kònatè.
Gaining power is not easy! (Indeed)

Ah! Bèmba! (Indeed)
The mother of King Dankaran Tuman, (Indeed)
When the Wizard had left the bush, (Indeed)
And offered his flesh-and-blood-brother the tail, (Indeed)
And when he said, "Here take the tail,"
She retorted: "Your mother, Sugulun Kòndè, will take the tail! (Indeed)
"And your younger sister, Sugulun Kulukan, (Indeed)
"And your younger brother, Manden Bukari. (Indeed)
"Go and seek a place to die, (Indeed)
"If not, I will chop through your necks,
"Cutting a handspan down into the ground.
"Be it so; you'll never return to the Manden again." (Indeed)
Son-Jara bitterly wept, bilika bilika! (Indeed)
And went to tell his mother. (Indeed)
His mother said, (Indeed)
"Ah! My child, (Indeed)
"Be calm. Salute your brother. (Indeed)
"Had he banished you as a cripple,
"Where would you have gone?
"Let us at least agree on that.
"Let us depart.
"What sitting will not solve,
"Travel will resolve." (That's true)

Episode Five: Mèma

They rose up. (Mmm)
The Kuyatè matriarch took up the iron rasp. (Mmm)
She sang a hunter's song for Nare Magan Kònatè:
"Took up the bow! (Indeed)
"Simbon, Master-of-the-Bush!
"Took up the bow!
"Took up the bow! (Indeed)
"Simbon, Master-of-Wild-Beasts!
"Took up the bow! (Indeed)
"Took up the bow! (Indeed)
"Warrior and Master-of-Slaves!
"Took up the bow! (Indeed)
"The Kòndè woman's child,
"Answerer-of-Needs, (Indeed)
"Took up the bow. (Indeed)

"Sugulan's Ma'an took up the bow. (Indeed)
You seized him, O Lion! (Indeed)
"And the Wizard killed him!
"O Simbon, that, the sound of your chords." (True)

He fled from suffering (Mmm)
To seek refuge with the blacksmith patriarch, (Indeed)
Because of the hardships of rivalry. (Mmm)
But they counted out one measure of gold, (Mmm)
And gave it to the blacksmith patriarch, (Indeed)
Saying, were he not to cast the Wizard out, (Indeed)
Saying, he would jeopardize the land, (Indeed)
Saying, the Manden would be the Wizard's, (Indeed)
Because of the hardships of rivalry. (Indeed)
The Wizard fled anew from suffering. (Mmm)
He went to seek refuge with the Karanga patriarch. (Indeed)
Do you not know that person's name? (Mmm)
Jobi, the Seer. (Indeed)
The Karanga patriarch was Jobi, the Seer. (I did not know that until you told me)

That Jobi, the Seer, (Indeed)
Married Sika Danba,
And fathered Sika Jata. (Indeed)
Sika Jata begat the Kònatè of Dabakala.
He was the Karanga ancestor. (Indeed)
A group of jinns was at the top of Genu mountain. [?] (Indeed)
From the time the sun set,
Until the next sun rose, (Indeed)
The brave jinns readied themselves.
They took a basket of millet seed, (Indeed)
And gave it to the Karanga patriarch,
Saying, he should settle in Bisan-dugu,
Saying, he should cultivate the land.

Because of the hardships of rivalry, (Indeed)
He cast the Wizard out. (Indeed)
He went then to seek refuge with Tulumbèn, King of Kòlè. (Indeed)

Because of the hardships of rivalry,

They counted out one measure of gold, (Mmm)
To give to King Tulumbèn of Kòlè.
Were he not to cast the Wizard out, (Mmm)
He would jeopardize Manden country,
Since the folk had lost their faith in him. (That's true)

He went to seek refuge
With the patriarch of the Magasubaas in Sigiri. (That's true)
The Jane patriarch, Bukari Jane, the Pure, made his ḥājj. (Indeed)
He entrusted his pregnant wife
To the patriarch of the Magasubaa, Tulunbèn, King of Kòlè.
And went forth upon his ḥājj. (Indeed)
He went forth to make the ḥājj. (Mmm)
Now, Magan Son-Jara had this fetish, (Mmm)
A fetish accepting no offering,
Unless, if a woman grow great with child, (Indeed)
The unborn babe be that offering. (Eh, Fa-Digi)
And Bukari Jane, the Pure, was making his ḥājj. (That's true)
He had entrusted his pregnant wife, (That's true)
To the patriarch of the Sigiri Magasubaa, Tulunbèn, King of Kòlè.
Bukari Jane, the Pure, (Indeed)
They slew his wife, (Mmm)
And offered the babe to the fetish,
And then gave it to Son-Jara,
So he could go seek refuge
With the nine Queens-of-Darkness,
Saying, the Manden would thus be his. (That's true)

Three days after this,
The holy-man returned from his ḥājj.
When night had reached its midpoint, (Indeed)
Having said his pair of litanies:
"Ah! God!
"What have I done to Thee? (Indeed)
"Alas, for pagans to slay my wife,
"And to make an offering of her babe,
"And to give it to some person,
"In his search for power,
"What have I done to Thee?"
And God carried on from there, (Indeed)

And cast a chain round the neck (Indeed)
Of that Tulunbèn, King of Kòlè, (Indeed)
And cast a chain round his right arm, (Indeed)
And cast one round his left, (Indeed)
And raised Tulunbèn, King of Kòlè, (Indeed)
Up between heaven and earth. (Mmm)
The lake in which he was sent splashing down,
Fikiri! (Mmm)
This is what is meant by Lowering-by-Chain.

That is what happened to the Sigiri Magasubaa patriarch. (Mmm)
Biribiriba went on to seek refuge
With the nine Queens-of-Darkness.
"What brought you here?" they asked of him. (Mmm)
"Have you not heard that none come here? (Indeed)
"What brought you here?" (Indeed)
The Sorcerer spoke out,
"Ah! Those who are feared by all,
"If you join them, you are spared.
"It is that which made me come here."
He sat down. (Indeed)
His flesh-and-blood-elder, King Dankaran Tuman, (Indeed)
He took his first-born daughter, (Indeed)
Caress-of-Hot-Fire, (Indeed)
And gave her to the Kuyatè patriarch, Dòka the Cat, (Indeed)
Saying, "Give her to Susu Mountain Sumamuru," (Indeed)
Saying, "Should he not slay the King of Nyani,"
Saying, "He's gone to seek refuge with the nine Queens-of-Darkness,"
Saying, "The folk have lost their faith in him." (True)

At that time, the bards did not have balaphones, (True)
Nor had the smiths a balaphone,
Nor had the funès a balaphone,
Nor did the cordwainers have one, (Indeed)
None but Susu Mountain Sumamuru. (Indeed)
  Sori Kantè the Tall, (Indeed)
  Who begat Bala Kantè of Susu, (Indeed)
  And who begat Kabani Kantè, (True)
  And who begat Kankuba Kantè,

And who begat Susu Mountain Sumamuru Kantè.
The village where Sumamuru was,
That village was called Dark Forest. (True)

It was there he came forth, my father, (Indeed)
Ah! Bèmba! (Indeed)
He came in Sumamuru's absence, (Indeed)
Dòka the Cat, (Indeed)
He asked for Sumamuru. (Indeed)
They said, "If you seek Sumamuru,
"Ask of the hawk!" (Mmm)
The balaphone of seven keys, (Mmm)
After Sumamuru had played that balaphone, (Indeed)
The mallets of the balaphone he would take,
And give them to the hawk. (Indeed)
It would fly up high in a Flame Tree,
And there in the depths of Susu Forest sit. (Indeed)
Dòka the Cat called to the hawk. (Indeed)
The balaphone mallets it delivered to him. (Indeed)
"Dun Fayiri, Nun Fayiri! (Indeed)
"Manda Kantè and Sama Kantè! (Indeed)
"Sori Kantè, the Tall! (Mmm)
"Susu Mountain Sumamuru Kantè! (Indeed)
"Salute Sumamuru! (Indeed)
"Sumamuru came amongst us,
"His pants of human skin. (Indeed)
"Sumamuru came amongst us,
"His coat of human skin. (Indeed)
"Sumamuru came amongst us,
"His helm of human skin. (Indeed)
"The first and ancient king,
"The King of yesteryear. (Indeed)
"So, respite does not end resolve.
"Sumamuru, I found you gone.
"Oh! Glorious Janjon!"

Sumamuru was off doing battle,
With pants of human skin,
And coat of human skin.
Whenever he would mount a hill,
Down another he would go.
Up one and down another.
Was it God or man?

He approached the Kuyatè patriarch, Dòka the
Cat: (Mmm)
"God or man?" (Indeed)
"I am a man," the reply.
"Where do you hail from?" (Mmm)
"I come," he said, "from the Manden. (Indeed)
"I am from Nyani." (Indeed)

"Play something for me to hear," he said. (Indeed)
He took up the balaphone: (Indeed)
"Kukuba and Bantanba!
"Nyani-nyani and Kamasiga!
"Brave child of the warrior!
"And Deliverer-of-the-Benign.
"Sumamuru came amongst us
"With pants of human skin.
"Sumamuru came amongst us,
"With coat of human skin.
"Sumamuru came amongst us
"With helm of human skin.
"The first and ancient king,
"The king of yesteryear.
"So, respite does not end resolve!
"Sumamuru, I found you gone.
"Oh! Glorious Janjon!"

He said, "Ah! What is your name?"
"My name is Dòka, the Cat." (Mmm)
"Will you not remain with me?"
"Not I! Two kings I cannot praise.
"I am Son-Jara's bard.
"From the Manden I have come,
"And to the Manden I must return." (True)

He laid hold of the Kuyatè patriarch,
And severed both Achilles tendons,
And by the Susu balaphone set him. (Indeed)
"Now what is your name?" (Indeed)
"Dòka, the Cat is still my name." (Indeed)
"Dòka, the Cat will no longer do." (Indeed)
He drew water and poured it over his head, (Indeed)
And shaved it clean, (Indeed)
And gave him the name Bala Faseke Kuyatè.

That Bala Faseke Kuyatè, (Indeed)
He fathered three children, (Indeed)
Musa and Mansa Magan, (Indeed)
Making Baturu, the Holy his last-born son in the
  Manden. (Indeed)
Those were the Kuyatès.

And this by the hand of Sumamuru.
He sent forth a messenger,
Saying, "Go tell King Dankaran Tuman," (Indeed)
Saying, "If you kill your own vicious dog,"
Saying, "Another man's will surely bite you." (Indeed, that's the truth)

With this he declared war, my father,
And went forth from Susu.
Going to fall on King Dankaran Tuman, (Indeed)
Breaking the Manden like an old pot, (Indeed)
Breaking the Manden like an old gourd, (Indeed)
Slaying the nine and ninety Masters-of-Shadow,
Slaying the nine and ninety royal princes,
And ousting King Dankaran Tuman.
He fled to Nsèrè-kòrò,
Saying, "I was spared. (Indeed)
"From your torment, I was spared. (True)
"From death, I have been spared." (Indeed)
And thus he settled there.
The sons he there begat, my father, (Indeed)
They became the Kisi people.
They are all in Masanta.
They had come from the Manden.
Their family name, it is Gindo. (Indeed)

Ah! Bèmba! (Indeed)
O Biribiriba!
He put gourds in the mouths
  of the poor and the powerful.
This by the hand of Susu Mountain Sumamuru, (Indeed)
Saying each must speak into his gourd,

Saying there is no pleasure in weakness,
Saying the Manden was now his.

He summoned Kankira-of-Silver (Indeed)
And Kankira-of-Gold, (Indeed)
The latter, the Saginugu patriarch, (Indeed)
And one red bull did give to them, (Indeed)
Saying they should offer it
To the nine Queens-of-Darkness, (Indeed)
Asking them to slay Son-Jara, (Mmm)
That he not enter the Manden again,
To say that the Manden be his,
Saying they have slain the
nine and ninety Masters-of-Shadow,
Saying they have slain the nine and
ninety royal princes,
And put gourds o'er the mouths
of the poor and the powerful, (Indeed)
Saying that they should slay him, (Indeed)
So he not enter the Manden again (Mmm)
To say that the Manden be his. (Indeed)

Those messengers arrived. (Indeed)
They came upon the witches there: (Indeed)
"Ilu tuntun!" (Indeed)
The witches did not speak. (Mmm)
"Peace be unto you." (Mmm)
The witches did not speak.
"Alu tuntun!"
The witches did not speak.
"Peace be with you!"
The witches did not speak. (That's true)

"The slaughtered bull, (Indeed)
"Lay it out in nine piles." (Indeed)
Nakana Tiliba then said to the witches,
"Each must either take her own, (Indeed)
"Questions without end looking for trouble, (That's true)
"Then take the meat and be off, (Indeed)
"Or," Nakana Tiliba continued,
"You must not take the meat.
"O Son-Jara, (Indeed)
"A message has come from the Manden, (Indeed)

"From Susu Mountain Sumamuru, (Indeed)
"Saying to come and tell us, (Indeed)
"Saying we should slay you, (Indeed)
"So that you not enter the Manden again,
"Saying, the folk have lost their faith in you. (Indeed)
"Saying, he has slain the nine and ninety Masters-of-Shadow, (Indeed)
"Saying, he has slain the nine and ninety royal princes. (Indeed)
"Nine were the times he razed the Manden,
"And nine were the times he rebuilt it, (Indeed)
"Saying, he put gourds on the mouths of the poor and the powerful, (Indeed)
"Saying, all must speak into their gourds,
"Saying, there is no pleasure in weakness,
"Saying, he has ousted King Dankaran Tuman,
"Saying, who has fled to Nsèrè-kòrò,
"Saying, we should slay you,
"So that you not enter the Manden again,
"And that is the reason for this meat."
"Then kill me," his reply.
"A person flees to be spared,
"But should one not be spared, then kill me!" (True)

Biribiriba! (Mmm)
He went to the back of the house.
Into a lion he transformed himself, (Mmm)
A lion seizing no one,
Before he had sounded a roar. (Mmm)
He went and seized a buffalo,
And came back and laid it down,
And went and seized another,
And came and laid it down,
And went and seized another,
And came and laid it down.
"Nine water buffalos, nine witches! (Mmm)
"Each take your own!" (True)
The witches then replied to him,
"Let us hold a council.
"The town where people hold no council,
"There will living not be good."

They went to hold their council.
"From the Manden and its neighbors, (Indeed)
"All of it together, and only one red bull! (Indeed)
"Son-Jara, you alone, nine buffalos!
"It is to him the Manden must belong!
"Let us then release him!" (True)
They trimmed a branch of the custard apple tree: (Indeed)
"When you leave the land of the nine
Queens-of-Darkness, (Indeed)
"You will see no village, (Mmm)
"Until you see Jula Fundu, (Mmm)
"The original town of the Mossi patriarch, (Indeed)
"Jula Fundu and Wagadugu, (Indeed)
"In Mèma Farin Tunkara's land of Mèma."
They stacked the bull meat in one pile, (Mmm)
And upon it laid its skin,
And upon this placed its head. (Mmm)
"All of you witches, say your verses! (Indeed)

"All of you witches, read your signs!" (Indeed)
Nakana Tiliba,
From her head she took her scarf,
And tied three knots into it,
And laid it o'er the meat,
Saying, "Rise up!
"Kitibili Kintin! (Indeed)
" 'Twas a man that puts us in conflict.
"A matter of truth is not to be feared."
The bull rose up and stretched. (Mmm)
It bellowed to Muḥammad. (Mmm)
The Messenger of God was thus evoked. (That's true)

That bull rose up and stretched. (Indeed)
Ah! Bèmba! (Indeed)
Son-Jara came forth: (Indeed)
"O Kankira-of-Silver and Kankira-of-Gold, (Indeed)
"A messenger is not to be whipped. (Indeed)
"A messenger is not to be defiled. (Indeed)
"When you go forth from here,
"You should go tell Susu Mountain Sumamuru, (Indeed)
"When you go forth from here, (Indeed)
"You should go tell Susu Mountain Sumamuru: (Indeed)

" 'The cowherd offers naught of the cow,'
" 'But the milk of Friday past.'
" 'No matter how loving the wet nurse,'
" 'The child will never be hers.'
"Say, 'A child may be first-born, but that does not always make him the elder.'
"Say, 'Today may belong to some,'
" 'Tomorrow will belong to another.'
"Say, 'As you succeeded some,'
" 'So shall you have successors.'
"Say, 'I am off to seek refuge with Mèma's Prince Tunkara,'
" 'In the land of Mèma.' "

He took the shape of a hawk.
You took it, Nare Magan Kònatè.
Biribiriba and Bow-of-the-Bush . . . ,
. . . fled because of suffering.
Gaining power is not easy.

Ah! Bèmba!
Son-Jara went to seek refuge in Mèma,
In a town of the Tunkaras, my father, in Mèma. (Indeed)
Kabala Simbon, the Dugunò bard patriarch was summoned, (Indeed)
And given a pouch of gold,
And given a game called sigi.

Ah! Bèmba! (Indeed)
That sigi-game, (Indeed)
From that comes the wori-game. (Indeed)
From that comes the mperi-game. (Indeed)
From the mperi-game come checkers and cards, (Indeed)

And thus they gave him a sigi-game: (Indeed)
"When you arrive in Mèma, (Indeed)
"If Son-Jara calls out, (Indeed)
" 'Simbon the Elder has come!' (Indeed)
" 'Simbon the Elder has come!'
"You should say,
" 'Ah! My little brother,' (Indeed)
" 'God has made you like the beehive.' (Indeed)
" 'The eye of the enemy is on you.' (Indeed)
" 'The hand of the enemy cannot touch you.' (Indeed)

" 'Ah! My little brother,' (Indeed)
" 'God has given you the bards and the smiths.' (Indeed)
" 'My little brother, the Manden belongs to you.' "

Kabala Simbon rose up.
As they were entering Mèma,
Son-Jara and Manden Bukari were going to the
bush. (Indeed)
He exclaimed, "O my brother, Manden Bukari! (Indeed)
"Simbon the Elder has come! (Indeed)
"Simbon the Elder has come!" (Indeed)
"Ah! My little brother, (Indeed)
"God has made you like the beehive. (Indeed)
"The eye of the enemy is on you.
"The hand of the enemy cannot touch you.
"Ah, my little brother,
"God has given you the bards and the smiths. (Indeed)
"Son-Jara, the Manden belongs to you!" (True)

He went then and gave the pouch of gold
To the Tunkara Patriarch, Prince Tunkara of
Mèma, (Indeed)
Saying they should cast the sigi. (Indeed)
When Son-Jara returned from the bush . . . , (Indeed)
Since Son-Jara entered Mèma, (Indeed)
The eldest Tunkara daughter had loved him. (Indeed)
Don't you know that person's name? (Indeed)
Her name was Mèma Sira.

Mèma Sira, (Indeed)
She saw these instructions take place:
"When dawn would break on the morrow,
"Son-Jara,
"He must cast the sigi with Prince Birama. (Indeed)
"If he cannot answer the sigi,"
Said, "Then you should slay the Sorcerer,
"So that he not enter the Manden again."
Said, "The folk have lost their faith in him." (Indeed)

Haven't you heard the sigi formula? (Indeed)
"Should Farin Birama take the sigi:
"Watarawaa! (Indeed)
"Should you be sent to slay your father, (Indeed)

"Then you must slay your father. (Indeed)
"Watarawaa! (Indeed)
"Should you be sent to slay your mother, (Indeed)
"Then you must slay your mother. (Indeed)
"Watarawaa!
"The commission you were sent for,
"You must see it through.
"O sigi, you must stand: nderen!
"That being done,
"The sigi will stand.

"Should Son-Jara not answer the sigi like this:
"Watarawaa! (Indeed)
"Faringa! (Indeed)
"Nkuramè!
"Should you be sent to slay your father, (Indeed)
"You must let him go! (Indeed)
"Watarawaa! (Indeed)
"Faringa! (Indeed)
"Nkuramè!
"Should you be sent to slay your mother,
"You must let her go!
"Watarawaa!
"Faringa!
"Nkuramè!
"If the people are to reject me,
"You must refuse your reward.
"O sigi, you must stand: jòn jòn jòn!
"Should that be done,
"The sigi will stand."
Said, "If he does not say that,"
Said, "Then he should be slain,"
Said, "So in the Manden he will not be killed."

O Biribiriba!
When the night had reached its midpoint: lelelele.
On that, Mèma Sira rose up, my father,
And laid her hand on the King of Nyani:
"Rise up, O King of Nyani. (Indeed)
"King of Nyani with helm of mail,
"He says he fears no man.
"Will you not rise up?
"Rise up, O King of Nyani!

"Rise up, O King of Nyani! (Indeed)
"An arrow at your right hand.
"Should someone pass you on the right,
"That is the arrow to slay him.
"An arrow at the Nyani King's left, (Indeed)
"Should you pass him on the left,
"That is the arrow to slay you.
"An arrow o'er the Nyani King's head,
"Should you pass o'er his head,
"That is the arrow to slay you.
"An arrow to the Nyani King's front,
"Should you pass before him,
"That is the arrow to slay you.
"Rise then, O King of Nyani! (Indeed)
"An arrow to the Nyani King's back, (Indeed)
"Should a person pass behind him,
"That is the arrow to slay him.
"Rise then, King of Nyani!
"O Wizard, won't you rise? (Indeed)
"A message has come from the Manden, (Indeed)
"That a pouch of gold be given my father, (Indeed)
"And a game called sigi. (Indeed)
"Tomorrow,
"You and my father must cast the sigi, (Indeed)
"Should you not answer the sigi,
"My father will then slay you,
"That you not enter the Manden again.
"O Nare Magan Kònatè!
"O Sorcerer-Seizing-Sorcerer!

"When my father takes the sigi: (Indeed)
"Watarawaa!
"Should you be sent to slay your father.
"You must slay your father, (Indeed)
"Watarawaa!
"Should you be sent to slay your mother,
"You must slay your mother. (Indeed)
"Watarawaa! (Indeed)
"The commission you were sent for,
"You must see it through!
"O sigi you must stand!
"Faringa!
"Nkuramè!

"When my father has said that, (Indeed)
"Should you not take the sigi:
"Watarawaa!
"Faringa!
"Nkuramè!
"Should you be sent to slay your father,
"You must let him go! (Indeed)
"Watarawaa!
"Faringa!
"Nkuramè!
"Should you be sent to slay your mother,
"You must let her go!
"Watarawaa!
"Faringa!
"Nkuramè!
"If the people are to reject me,
"You must refuse your reward.
"O sigi, you must stand: jòn jòn jòn!
"Should you not say that,
"My father will then slay you,
"That you not enter the Manden again."

O Biribiriba!
When the day had dawned, (Mmm)
Prince Birama let loose the royal drum, (Indeed)
The drum of power: (Indeed)
"Like-It-Or-Not."
That is the tabule's sound. (Indeed)
All thus found themselves together. (Indeed)
He cast the sigi. (Indeed)
The Sorcerer answered the sigi. (Indeed)
Kabala Simbon, the Dugunò bard patriarch said, (Indeed)
"The message entrusted to me,
"That message is this: (Indeed)
" 'Let the Wizard go,
" 'The Manden belongs to him.' "
. . .

Bèmba!
Biribiriba!
Nare Magan Kònatè! (Indeed)
The bards sing thus of the Sorcerer,

Nare Magan Kònatè!
Sorcerer-Seizing-Sorcerer! (Indeed)
Kala Jula Sangoyi Mamunaka!

Son-Jara cast the sigi. (Indeed)
Kabala Simbon, the Dugunò bard patriarch, (Indeed)
Prince Birama beheld Kabala Simbon, (Indeed)
"Let the Wizard go," he said. (Indeed)
"The Manden belongs to him." (Indeed)

Kabala Simbon, the Dugunò bard patriarch, (Indeed)
He went back to the Manden, (Indeed)
And told Susu Mountain Sumamuru,
Saying that Son-Jara was in Mèma, (Indeed)
No harm had come to Nare Magan Kònatè, (Indeed)
To Simbon, Lion-Born-of-the-Cat. (That's the truth)
Son-Jara's flesh-and-blood-sister, Kankuba Kantè, (Indeed)
His flesh-and-blood-sister, Sugulun Kòndè, (Indeed)
That Sugulun Kòndè, (Indeed)
She stripped off that gourd from Fa-Koli's mouth, (Indeed)
Stripped off that gourd from Tura Magan's mouth, (Indeed)
Stripped off that gourd from Sira's mouth, the Jawara patriarch. (Indeed)
On that, those people rose up, my father, (Indeed)
With cotton seeds, (Indeed)
With fresh okra, (Indeed)
And flour of eggplant leaf. (Indeed)
They set forth to Mèma, (That's the truth)
In search of Nare Magan Kònatè. (Indeed, indeed, indeed)

It was market day in Mèma. (Indeed)
They went there to market their goods. (Indeed)
A woman bought the fresh okra (Indeed)
And the flour of eggplant leaf, (Indeed)
And brought it back to Sugulun Kòndè. (Indeed)
The old Kòndè woman was in her hut. (That's the truth)
"We have seen some things today. (Indeed)
"We know not of their essence." (Indeed)
The Kòndè woman sniffed of it. (Indeed)
"Whatever this may be, (Indeed)
"From the Manden it has come.
"From whosoever's hand this came,
"Summon those people here! (Indeed)

"This has come from the Manden!" (Indeed)
They summoned Tura-Magan,
And Bee-King-of-the-Wilderness, (Indeed)
And Fa-Kanda Tunandi, (Indeed)
And Sura, the Jawara patriarch. (Indeed)
They summoned Tura-Magan-and-Kanke-jan. (Indeed)
They came forward. (Indeed)
The Kòndè woman spoke out: (Indeed)
"The quiver-bearers have come!
"The bow-bearers have come!
"Greetings on your arrival! (Mmm, indeed)
"Ah! Taraweres! (Indeed)
"How do the folk of the Manden fare? (Indeed)
"Greetings on your arrival! (Indeed)
"How do the folk of the Manden fare?" (Indeed)

Biribiriba, the Wizard was in the bush. (Indeed)
His flesh-and-blood-sister Sugulun Kòndè, . . . (Indeed)
Son-Jara had killed nine buffaloes, (Indeed)
And one club rat. (Indeed)
His flesh-and-blood-sister, Sugulun Kòndè, (Indeed)
She took the buffalo hearts, (Indeed)
And also took their livers. (Indeed)
And that meat had yet to be butchered, (Indeed)
And took the club rat, (Indeed)
And cooked it up with the rice. (Indeed)
When the meat was being butchered, (Indeed)
Manden Bukari saw no hearts,
Nor did he see any livers. (Indeed)
He said: "Ah, my elder brother (Indeed)
"This buffalo has no heart,
"Nor does it have a liver!" (Indeed)
"My little brother," the reply, (Indeed)
"Let us be off for home. (Indeed)
"You will find strangers come in our
absence." (That's the truth)
Ah, Bards! He who would cultivate,
Let him cultivate! (Indeed)
Son-Jara is done! (Yes, Fa-Digi)
He who would deal in commerce,
Let him deal in commerce! (Indeed)
Cultivating is suitable to some,
Commerce does not suit them. (That's the truth)

Commerce is suitable to some,
Cultivation does not suit them. (Indeed)
This was sung at Son-Jara's tomb,
By the Manden Sankarandin, (That's the truth)
The name of the village was Nyani, (Indeed)
On the banks of the Sankarandin. (Indeed)
Joma, the Smooth and Joma, the Rough. (Indeed)
On each bank of the river there,
They were all of royal clan. (Indeed)
Gaining power is not easy! (That's the truth)

O Garan! (Indeed)
The mastersingers sing of Biribiriba,
Of Nare Magan Kònatè! (Indeed)
O King of Nyani! King of Nyani! (Indeed)
King of Nyani with helm of mail,
He says he fears no man.
Have no fear!
Powerlessness and rivalry are not the same. (That's the truth)
King of Nyani! King of Nyani! (Indeed)
King of Nyani with shirt of mail,
He says he fears no man.
Have no fear! (Indeed)
Powerlessness and rivalry are not the same. (That's the truth)
O Biribiriba, the mastersingers call upon you. (Indeed)
O Nare Magan Kònatè,
O Sorcerer-Seizing-Sorcerer. (Indeed, yes, yes, yes, yes)

Ah! Garan! (Indeed)
They left the bush. (Indeed)
They came back home. (Indeed)
Sugulun Kulunkan brought out the rice, (Indeed)
And came to set it down. (Indeed)
The meat lay upon it. (Indeed)

Her flesh-and-blood-brother Manden Bukari raged. (Indeed)
It was he after all had suffered the hunger. (Indeed)
It was he after all had suffered the thirst, (Indeed)
And undergone those hardships, (Indeed)
Having gone into the bush, (Indeed)
And having suffered the misery, (Indeed)

And having endured the gnats, (Indeed)
And the dreadful deerflies! (Indeed)
"If all of that be true,"
Said, "Let the meat rise from the rice!"
The club rat rose up off the rice, (Indeed)
And ran toward the door of the hut, (Indeed)
Fixing its eyes on the King of Nyani: (Indeed)
"O Kòndè woman's child, Answerer-of-Needs!" (Indeed)

It fixed its eyes upon them thus: (Indeed)
"Simbon, Lion-Born-of-the-Cat! (Indeed)
"Nare Magan Kònatè!" (Yes, yes, yes, yes, yes, yes, yes)

It fixed its eyes upon the King of Nyani:
"O Sorcerer-Seizing-Sorcerer!" (Indeed)
His little sister then spoke up:
"Ah, my elder brother, (Indeed)
"I took the buffalo hearts and livers. (Indeed)
"I did not take them to please a lover. (Indeed)
"I did not take them to please myself. (Indeed)
"The breast that Son-Jara once did suckle, (Indeed)
"When the Wizard gave it up, (Indeed)
"It was you who then did take it. (Indeed)
"When you did give it up, (Indeed)
"It was I who then did take it, my father. (Indeed)
"The dishonor bound for Son-Jara, (Indeed)
"That dishonor did I avert. (Indeed)
"If all of that be true, (Indeed)
"Then let the meat lie on the rice!" (Indeed)
The meat lay back upon the rice. (Indeed)
She invited, "Come and eat!" (Indeed)
  O Nare Magan Kònatè!
  Sorcerer-Seizing-Sorcerer! (Indeed, eh, Fa-Digi)

Manden Bukari cursed Sugulun Kulunkan. (Indeed)
The seven skirts about her waist,
All those skirts fell off save her slip. (Indeed)
She said, "Ah, my elder brother, (Indeed)
"No good can come from a curse. (Indeed)
"Cursing an elder can bring no good.
"Were that not so, I would curse you, (Indeed)
"But, each of your descendants, (Indeed)
"No powder will they here discharge, (Indeed)

"No rifle of war will they fire again!" (Indeed)
And his descendants became the people of
Hamina. (Indeed)
O Nare Magan Kònatè!
O Sorcerer-Seizing-Sorcerer! (Indeed)

Those were the descendants of Manden Bukari.
They can be found in Hamina. (Indeed)
Ah! God is the King.
God has the power (Indeed)
To render some folk wealthy,
Yet they do naught for Him, (Indeed)
And some to render destitute, (Indeed)
And yet they did naught to Him. (Indeed)
God is the King! (Indeed)
. . . (Indeed)
O Nare Magan Kònatè!
O Sorcerer-Seizing-Sorcerer! (Indeed)

O Garan! (Indeed)
O Sangoyi! (Indeed)
God is the King!
A man of power . . . (That's the truth)
Mansa Magan came for me, (Indeed)
A letter was given to me,
Saying I should speak on Radio Mali,
To sing the praise of Fa-Koli. (Indeed, that happened!
That really happened!)

I was there at my farming village, (Indeed)
In brotherhood and affection. (Indeed)
Mansa Magan came to get me, my father,
Saying I should sing for the whiteman. (Indeed)
God is the King! (That's the truth)

O Garan! (Indeed)
O Great-Host-Slaying-Stranger and the
Twisted Well. (Indeed)
And the Devourers-of-the-Knowing! (Indeed)
The explanations were made to the Wizard, (Indeed)
To Nare Magan Kònatè. (Indeed)
Son-Jara had a certain fetish, (Indeed)
Accepting no sacrifice save shea butter. (Indeed)
There were no shea trees there in Mèma. (Indeed)

O Mansa Magan! (Indeed)
Wherever you sacrifice to the shea tree, (Indeed)
That town must be in Mandenland. (Indeed)

All of them are in the Manden. (Indeed)
No shea trees were there in Mèma, (Indeed)
Save one old dry Shea tree in Mèma. (Indeed)
Son-Jara's mother came forward: (Indeed)
"Ah! God! (Indeed)
"Let Son-Jara go to the Manden. (Indeed)
"He is the man for the morrow. (Indeed)
"He is the man for the day to follow. (Indeed)
"He is to rule o'er the bards, (Indeed)
"He is to rule o'er the smiths, (Indeed)
"And the three and thirty warrior clans. (Indeed)
"He will rule o'er all those people. (Indeed)
"Ah, God! (Indeed)
"Before the break of day, (Indeed)
"That dried up shea tree here, (Indeed)
"Let it bear leaf and fruit. (Indeed)
"Let the fruit fall down to earth, (Indeed)
"So that Son-Jara may gather the fruit,
"From it to make shea butter, (Indeed)
"To offer his fetish. (Indeed, yes, Fa-Digi)

"Ah, God! (Indeed)
"Let Son-Jara go to the Manden. (Indeed)
"He is the man for the morrow.
"He is the man for the day to follow. (Indeed)
"He will rule the bards and smiths. (Indeed)
"The Manden belongs to the Wizard. (Indeed)
"Before the break of day, (Indeed)
"Let me change my dwelling, (Indeed)
"Old am I and cannot travel. (Indeed)
"Let Nare Magan Kònatè go home." (Indeed)
When the day was dawning, (Indeed)
The dried up shea tree did bear leaf. (Indeed)
Its fruit did fall to earth. (Indeed)
Son-Jara looked in on the Kòndè woman, (Indeed)
But the Kòndè woman had abandoned the world. (Indeed)
He washed his mother's body, (Indeed)
And then he dug her grave, (Indeed)
And wrapped her in a shroud, (Indeed)
And laid his mother in the earth, (Indeed)

And then chopped down a kapok tree, (Indeed)
And wrapped it in a shroud, (Indeed)
And laid it in the house, (Indeed)
And laid a blanket over it, (Indeed)
And sent a messenger to Prince Birama,
Asking of him a grant of land, (Indeed)
In order to bury his mother in Mèma,
So that he could return to the Manden. (Indeed)
This answer they did give to him
That no land could he have,
Unless he were to pay its price. (Indeed)

Prince Birama decreed, (Indeed)
Saying he could have no land, (Indeed)
Unless he were to pay its price. (Indeed)
He took feathers of Guinea fowl and partridge, (Indeed)
And took some leaves of arrow-shaft plant, (Indeed)
And took some leaves of wild grass reed, (Indeed)
And took some red fanda-vines, (Indeed)
And took one measure of shot, (Indeed)
And took a haftless knife, (Indeed)
And added a cornerstone fetish to that, (Indeed)
And put it all in a leather pouch, (Indeed)
Saying go give it to Prince Birama, (Indeed)
Saying it was the price of his land. (Indeed, ha, Fa-Digi)

That person gave it to Prince Birama. (Indeed)
Prince Birama summoned his three sages, (Indeed)
All-Knowing-Sage, (Indeed)
All-Seeing-Sage, (Indeed)
All-Saying-Sage. (Indeed)
The three sages counseled Prince Birama. (Indeed)
He said, "O Sages! (Indeed)
"The forest by the river is never empty. [?] (Indeed)
"You also should take this. (Indeed)
"That which came first, (Indeed)
"I will not take it. (Indeed)
"Tis yours." (Indeed)
O Garan! (Indeed)
All-Seeing-Sage,
All-Saying-Sage,
All-Knowing-Sage, (Indeed)
They untied the mouth of the pouch,
And shook its contents out. (Indeed)

The All-Seeing-Sage exclaimed, (Indeed)
"Anyone can see that! (Indeed)
"I am going home!" (Indeed)
The All-Knowing-Sage exclaimed, (Indeed)
"Everybody knows that! (Indeed)
"I am going home." (Indeed)
All-Saying-Sage exclaimed, (Indeed)
"Everyone knows that? (Indeed)
"That is a lie! (Indeed)
"Everyone sees that? (Indeed)
"That is a lie! (Indeed)
"There may be something one may see,
"Be it ne'er explained to him,
"He will never know it. (Indeed)

"Prince Birama, (Indeed)
"Did you not see feathers of Guinea fowl and partridge?
"They are the things of ruins. (Indeed)
"Did you not see the leaf of arrow-shaft plant?
"That is a thing of ruins. (Indeed)
"Was not your eye on the wild grass reed? (Indeed)
"That is a thing of ruins. (Indeed)
"Did you not see those broken shards? (Indeed)
"They are the things of ruins. (Indeed)
"Did you not see that measure of shot? (Indeed)
"The annihilator of Mèma! (Indeed)
"Did you not see that haftless knife? (Indeed)
"The warrior-head-severing blade! (Indeed)
"Was not your eye on the red fanda-vine? (Indeed)
"The warrior-head-severing blood! (Indeed)
"If you do not give the land to him, (Indeed)
"That cornerstone fetish your eye beheld,
"It is the warrior's thunder shot! (Indeed)
"If you do not give the land to him,
"To Nare Magan Kònatè,
"The Wizard will reduce the town to ruin. (Indeed)
"Son-Jara is to return to the Manden!" (That's the truth)

They gave the land to the Sorcerer, (Indeed)
He buried his mother in Mèma's earth.
He rose up.
That which sitting will not solve,
Travel will resolve. (Indeed)

Episode Six: Kulu-Kòrò

The Kuyatè matriarch took the iron rasp,
And sang a hunter's song behind him: (Indeed)
"Took up the bow, (Indeed)
"Simbon, Master-of-the-Bush
"Took up the bow!
"Took up the bow! (Indeed)
"Simbon, Master-of-the-Beasts (Indeed)
"Took up the bow! (Indeed)
"Took up the bow! (Indeed)
"Ruler of the bards and smiths,
"Took up the bow!
"The Kòndè woman's child,
"Answerer-of-Needs (Indeed)
"Took up the bow! (Indeed)
"Sugulun's Ma'an took up the bow! (Indeed)
"You seized him, O Lion! (Indeed)
"The sorcerer slew him.
"Simbon, 'tis the sound of your chords!" (Indeed)

Biribiriba rose up,
And went to find the Dabò patriarch. (Indeed)
He was sitting at the crossroads boiling a potion. (Indeed)
It was the voice of the Dabò patriarch: (Indeed)
"Sorcerer, let us play awhile the warrior game!" (Indeed)
He made Son-Jara fall to his right. (Indeed)
Said the Tarawere patriarch, Tura-Magan-and-Kanke-jan:
"Let us abandon Son-Jara. (Indeed)
"This person that Dabò has thrown, (Indeed)
"Given that, if we not abandon him, (Indeed)
"Were we to go to the Manden,
"Sumamuru would destroy our folk!" (Indeed)
Son-Jara was enraged at that, (Indeed)
And jamming his foot on Dabò's instep,
He stretched him out by the neck, (Indeed)
Ripping off his head. (Indeed)
The clamor, "A d'a bò! He ripped it off! (Indeed)
Thus, that became the Dabò surname. (Indeed, that's the truth)
He fled because of suffering! (Indeed)
O Biribiriba! (Indeed)
When he and his mother were going to Mèma, (Indeed)

She took her silver bracelet off,
And gave it to the Boatman patriarch,
To Sasagalò, the Tall. (Indeed)
The ancestor of the boatman was Sasagalò, the Tall.
She took her silver bracelet off: (Indeed)
"When one digs a distant-day well,
"Should a distant-day thirst descend, then drink!" (Indeed)

A partridge was sent to deliver the message (Indeed)
To Susu Mountain Sumamuru: (Indeed)
"Manda and Sama Kantè! (Indeed)
"Susu Bala Kantè!
"Kukuba and Bantanba!
"Nyani-nyani and Kamasiga! (Indeed)
"Brave child of the warrior!
"And Deliverer-of-the-Benign!
"Sumamuru came among us
"With pants of human skin! (Indeed)
"Sumamuru came among us
"With coat of human skin. (Indeed)
"Applaud him! (Indeed)
"Susu Mountain Sumamuru!
"The Sorcerer with his army has left Mèma. (Indeed)
"He has entered the Manden!" (Indeed)

Susu Mountain Sumamuru, (Indeed)
He took four measures of gold, (Indeed)
To the Boatman patriarch,
Sasagalò, the Tall, did give them, (Indeed)
Saying, "That army coming from Mèma, (Indeed)
"That army must not cross!" (Indeed)

For one entire month, (Indeed)
Son-Jara and his army by the riverbank sat. (Indeed)
He wandered up and down. (Indeed)
One day Son-Jara rose up
And followed up the river: (Indeed)
"Being good, a bane. (Indeed)
"Not being good, a bane. (Indeed)
"When my mother and I were going to Mèma, (Indeed)
"She took her silver bracelet off, (Indeed)
"And gave it to a person here, (Indeed)
"Saying when you dig a distant-day well,

"When a distant-day thirst descends, then drink. (Indeed)
"Thus have I come with my army, (Indeed)
"And we have not yet made a crossing." (Indeed)
The Boatman patriarch responded: (Indeed)
"Ah! Is it you who are Son-Jara?" (Indeed)
The reply, "It is I who am Son-Jara." (Indeed)
"You are Son-Jara?" (Indeed)
"Indeed I am Son-Jara!" (Indeed)
"It is you who are Nare Magan Kònatè? (Indeed)
"If God wills,
"With the break of day,
"Tomorrow will the army cross." (Indeed)

At the break of day, (Indeed)
The Boatman patriarch, Sasagalò the Tall, (Indeed)
He brought Son-Jara across. (Indeed)
The Wizard advanced with his army. (Indeed)
They fell upon Sumamuru at Dark Forest. (Indeed)
But he drove them off. (Indeed)
Susu Mountain Sumamuru drove Son-Jara off. (Indeed)
He went and founded a town called Anguish, (Indeed)
Of which the bards did sing:
"We will not move to Anguish. (Indeed)
"Should one go to Anguish,
"Should not anguish he endure, (Indeed)
"Then nothing would he reap. (Indeed)
"We will not move to Anguish." (Indeed)

That Anguish, (Indeed)
The Maninka sing this of it, my father:
"There is no joy in you." (Indeed)
Our name for that town is Anguish (Nyani). (Indeed)

The Wizard advanced with his army. (Indeed)
They went to fall on Susu Mountain Sumamuru. (Indeed)
He drove Son-Jara off again. (Indeed)
He went to found the town called Resolve. (Indeed)
The bards thus sing of it:
"We will not move to Resolve.
"Should one move to Resolve,
"Should not resolve he entertain,
"Then nothing would he reap. (Indeed)
"We will not move to Resolve." (Indeed)

The Wizard advanced again. (Indeed)
He with his bards advanced. (Indeed)
They went to fall on Susu Mountain Sumamuru. (Indeed)
Sumamuru drove him off with his bards. (Indeed)
They went to found the town called Sharing. (Indeed)
And they sang:
  "Let us move to the Wizard's town, my father.
  "To Sharing, (Indeed)
  "The town where sharing is not done,
  "Founding that town is not easy." (Indeed)
They went to found the town called Sharing. (Indeed)

Son-Jara's flesh-and-blood-sister, Sugulun
  Kulunkan, (Indeed)
She said, "O Magan Son-Jara, (Indeed)
"One person cannot fight this war. (Indeed)
"Let me go seek Sumamuru. (Indeed)
"Were I then to reach him,
"To you I will deliver him, (Indeed)
"So that the folk of the Manden be yours, (Indeed)
"And all the Mandenland you shield." (Indeed)
Sugulun Kulunkan arose, (Indeed)
And went up to the gates of Sumamuru's fortress: (Indeed)
  "Manda and Sama Kantè! (Indeed)
  "Kukuba and Bantamba
  "Nyani-nyani and Kamasiga! (Indeed)
  "Brave child of the Warrior,
  "And Deliverer-of-the-Benign. (Indeed)
  "Sumamuru came amongst us
  "With pants of human skin. (Indeed)
  "Sumamuru came amongst us
  "With shirt of human skin. (Indeed)
  "Sumamuru came amongst us
  "With helm of human skin. (Indeed)
"Come open the gates, Susu Mountain
  Sumamuru! (Indeed)

"Come make me your bed companion!" (Indeed)
Sumamuru came to the gates: (Indeed)
"What manner of person are you?" (Indeed)
"It is I Sugulun Kulunkan!" (Indeed)
"Well, now, Sugulun Kulunkan, (Indeed)

"If you have come to trap me, (Indeed)
"To turn me over to some person, (Indeed)
"Know that none can ever vanquish me. (Indeed)
"I have found the Manden secret, (Indeed)
"And made the Manden sacrifice, (Indeed)
"And in five score millet stalks placed it, (Indeed)
"And buried them here in the earth. (Indeed)
" 'Tis I who found the Manden secret, (Indeed)
"And made the Manden sacrifice, (Indeed)
"And in a red piebald bull did place it, (Indeed)
"And buried it here in the earth. (Indeed)
"Know that none can vanquish me. (Indeed)
" 'Tis I who found the Manden secret (Indeed)
"And made a sacrifice to it, (Indeed)
"And in a pure white cock did place it. (Indeed)
"Were you to kill it, (Indeed)
"And uproot some barren groundnut plants, (Indeed)
"And strip them of their leaves,
"And spread them round the fortress, (Indeed)
"And uproot more barren peanut plants, (Indeed)
"And fling them into the fortress, (Indeed)
"Only then can I be vanquished." (Indeed)
His mother sprang forward at that: (Indeed)
"Heh! Susu Mountain Sumamuru! (Indeed)
"Never tell all to a woman,
"To a one-night woman! (Indeed)
"The woman is not safe, Sumamuru." (Indeed)
Sumamuru sprang towards his mother, (Indeed)
And came and seized his mother, (Indeed)
And slashed off her breast with a knife, magasi! (Indeed)
She went and got the old menstrual cloth. (Indeed)
"Ah! Sumamuru!" she swore. (Indeed)
"If your birth was ever a fact,
"I have cut your old menstrual cloth!"

O Kalajula Sangoyi Mamunaka! (Indeed)
He lay Sugulun Kulunkan down on the bed. (Indeed)
After one week had gone by,
Sugulun Kulunkan spoke up: (Indeed)
"Ah, my husband, (Indeed)
"Will you not let me go to the Manden, (Indeed)
"That I may get my bowls and spoons,
"For me to build my household here?" (Indeed)

From that day to this,
Should you marry a woman in Mandenland, (Indeed)
When the first week has passed,
She will take a backward glance, (Indeed)
And this is what that custom means. (Yes, Fa-Digi, that's the truth)

Sugulun returned to reveal those secrets
To her flesh-and-blood-brother, Son-Jara. (Indeed)
The sacrifices did Son-Jara thus discover. (Indeed)
The sacrifices did he thus discover. (Indeed)
Now five score wives had Susu Mountain
Sumamuru, (Indeed)
One hundred wives had he. (Indeed)
His nephew, Fa-Koli, had but one, (Indeed)

. . . (Mmm)
And Sumamuru, five score! (Indeed)
When a hundred bowls they would cook
To make the warriors' meal, (Indeed)
Fa-Koli's wife alone would one hundred cook
To make the warriors' meal, (That's the truth, eh, Fa-Digi, indeed, indeed)
"Let the fonio increase! (Indeed)
"Let the rice increase! (Indeed)
"Let the groundnuts increase! (Indeed)
"Let the groundpeas increase! (Indeed)
"Let the beans increase!" (Indeed)
She took them all one by one, (Indeed)
And put them all in one pot, (Indeed)
And in that pot they all were cooked, (Indeed)
And served it all in her calabash, (Indeed)
And all of this for Fa-Koli. (Indeed)
. . .
[Sumamuru takes Fa-Koli's wife from him.]
. . .

Ah! Garan! (Indeed)
[Fa-Koli leaves Sumamuru and comes to Son-Jara's camp.]
. . .
. . .
Hero-of-the-Original-Clans and Magan
Sukudana! (Indeed)
Son-Jara called out, (Indeed)

"Who in the Manden will make this sacrifice?" (Indeed)
"I shall!" Fa-Koli's reply. (Indeed)
"The thing that drove me away, (Indeed)
"And took my only wife from me,
"So that not even a weak wife have I now, (Indeed)
"I shall make the whole sacrifice!" (Indeed)
Fa-Koli thus made the whole sacrifice. (Indeed)
He came and reported to the Wizard.
Son-Jara then called out: (Indeed)
"Who will bring us face to face,
"That we may join in battle?" (Indeed)
"I shall," Fa-Koli's reply. (Indeed)
On that Fa-Koli rose up. (Indeed)
He arrived in Dark Forest. (Indeed)
As he espied the rooftops of Sumamuru's city, Dark
  Forest, (Indeed)
With every single step he took, (Indeed)
He thrust a dart into the earth, (Indeed)
And in a tree fork laid another. (Indeed, yes, Fa-Digi)
With every single step he took, (Indeed)
He thrust a dart into the earth, (Indeed)
And in a tree fork laid another, (That's the truth)
Until he entered the very gates,
Until he entered the city. (Indeed)
O, Garan! (Indeed)
The daughter given by King Dankaran Tuman, (Indeed)
Given to Susu Mountain Sumamuru, (Indeed)
That he should go and kill Son-Jara, (Indeed)
Fa-Koli went and seized that maiden, (Indeed)
"Come! Your uncle has left Mèma! (Indeed)
"Your uncle has summoned you. (Indeed)
"Your uncle has now come. He has left Mèma!" (Indeed)
The people of Susu pursued them: biri biri biri. (Indeed)
They came attacking after them: yrrrrrrr! (Indeed)
With every single step he took, (Indeed)
He drew a war dart from the earth,
And hurled it at the Susu, (Indeed)
And from a tree fork grabbed another, (Indeed)
And hurled it at the Susu, (Indeed)
"Heh! Come to my aid! (Indeed)
"Heaven and Earth, come aid me!
"Susu Mountain Sumamuru is after
  me!" (Indeed, yes, father)

He retreated on and on.
He drew a war dart from the earth,
And hurled it at the Susu, (Indeed)
And from a tree fork grabbed another, (Indeed)
And fired it at the Susu. (Indeed)
"Heh! Come to my aid! (Indeed)
"Heaven and Earth, come to my aid!
"Susu Mountain Sumamuru is after me!" (That's the truth)

At that, the Susu said, my father, (Indeed)
"If we do not fall back from Fa-Koli, (Indeed)
"Fa-Koli will bring all our folk to an end! (Indeed)
"Let us fall back from Fa-Koli! (Indeed)
    Hero-of-the-Original-Clans and Magan Sukudana.
    . . . (That's the truth)
And thus they fell back from Fa-Koli. (Indeed)
They readied themselves for battle. (Indeed)
Susu Mountain Sumamuru came forward, (Indeed)
And taking his favorite wife,
On the saddle's cantle sat her, (Indeed)
With golden ladle and silver ladle. (Indeed)
Son-Jara attacked and encircled the walls. (Indeed)
He had split the enemy army, (Indeed)
And taken the fortress gates. (Indeed)
Susu Mountain Sumamuru charged out at a gallop. (Indeed)
Fa-Koli, (Indeed)
With Tura-Magan-and-Kanke-jan, (Indeed)
And Bee-King-of-the-Wilderness, (Indeed)
And Fa-Kanda Tunandi, (Indeed)
And Sura, the Jawara patriarch, (Indeed)
And Son-Jara, (Indeed)
They all chased after Sumamuru. (True)
They arrived at Kukuba. (Indeed)
He told them, "I am not ready!" (Indeed)
They let him go: (Indeed)
"Prepare yourself!" (Indeed)
They arrived at Kamasiga, (Indeed)
"I am not ready." (Indeed)
They let him go: (Indeed)
"Prepare yourself!" (Indeed)
They arrived at Nyani-Nyani. (Indeed)
Said, "I am not ready." (Indeed)
They let him go again:

"Prepare yourself!" (Indeed)
They arrived at Bantanba, (Indeed)
"I am not ready." (Indeed)
And again they let him go:
"Prepare yourself!" (Indeed)
And still they attacked him from behind,
Behind Susu Mountain Sumamuru. (That's the truth,
yes, Fa-Digi)

Sumamuru crossed the river at Kulu-Kòrò, (Indeed)
And had his favored wife dismount, (Indeed)
And gave her the ladle of gold,
Saying that he would drink, (Indeed)
Saying else the thirst would kill him. (That's the truth)
The favored wife took the ladle of gold, (Indeed)
And filled it up with water, (Indeed)
And to Sumamuru stretched her hand,
And passed the water to him. (Indeed)
Fa-Koli with his darts charged up:
  "O Colossus, (Indeed)
  "We have taken you! (That's the truth)
  "We have taken you, Colossus!
  "We have taken you, Colossus!
  "We have taken you!" (Indeed)
Tura Magan held him at bladepoint. (Indeed)
Sura, the Jawara patriarch held him at bladepoint. (Indeed)
Fa-Koli came up and held him at bladepoint.
Son-Jara held him at bladepoint: (Indeed)
  "We have taken you, Colossus! (That's the truth)
  "We have taken you!" (Indeed)
Sumamuru dried up on the spot: nyònyòwu! (Indeed)
He has become the sacred fetish of Kulu-Kòrò. (Indeed)
The Bambara worship that now, my father.
Susu Mountain Sumamuru,
He became that sacred fetish. (That's the truth, indeed,
father, yes, yes, yes, yes)

Episode Seven: Kanbi

Biribiriba turned back, Son-Jara! (Indeed)
  Stranger-in-the-Morning, Chief-in-the-
    Afternoon! (Indeed)

Great-Host-Slaying-Stranger!
Stump-in-the-Dark-of-Night! (Indeed)
Should you bump against it,
It will bump against you! (That's the truth)
The Granary Guard Dog. (Indeed)
The thing discerning not the stranger,
Nor the familiar.
Should it come upon any person,
He will be bitten. (That's the truth)
Kirikara Watita! (Indeed)
Adversity's true place!
Man's reason and woman's are not the same.
Pretty words and truth are not the
same. (That's the truth)
No matter how long the road,
It always comes out at someone's home. (Indeed)
The Nyani king with his army came forward, (Indeed)
Saying the Manden belonged to him, (That's the truth)
Saying no more was he rival to any, (That's the truth)
Saying the Manden belonged to him. (That's the truth)

He found the Kuyatè patriarch with tendons cut, (Indeed)
And beckoned him to rise, "Let us go! (Indeed)
"Bala Faseke Kuyatè, arise. Let us go!" (Indeed)
He lurched forward, (Indeed)
Saying he would rise.
He fell back to the ground again, (Indeed)
His two Achilles tendons cut: (Indeed)
"O Nare Magan Kònatè!" (Indeed)
"Arise and let us go! (Indeed)
"I have no rival in Mandenland now! (That's the truth)
"The Manden is mine alone." (Indeed)
He lurched forward, (Indeed)
Saying that he would rise. (Indeed)
He fell back to the ground again. (Indeed)
"Had Sumamuru no child?" they queried. (Indeed)
"Here is his first born son," the reply. (Indeed)
"What is his name?" (Indeed)
"His name is Mansa Saman." (Indeed)
They summoned Mansa Saman (Indeed)
And brought forth Dòka the Cat,
And placed him on Mansa Saman's shoulders, (Indeed)

Laying the balaphone on his head, serew! (Indeed)
He followed after the Wizard: (Indeed)
"Biribiriba! (Indeed)
"O Nare Magan Kònatè! (Indeed)
"Entered Kaya,
"Son-Jara entered Kaya. (That's the truth)
"Entered Kaya,
"Sugulun's Ma'an entered Kaya. (Yes, Fa-Digi)
"If they took no gold, (Indeed)
"If they took no measure of gold for the Wizard, (Indeed)
"The reason for Son-Jara's coming to the Manden,
"To stabilize the Manden,
"To improve the people's lot: jon jon! (That's the truth)
"O Sorcerer, you have come for the Manden people! (Indeed)
"O Nare Magan Kònatè, (Indeed)
"O Khalif Magan Kònatè!" (That's the truth)
They arrived back in the Manden. (Indeed)
The Sorcerer ruled over everyone. (Indeed)
He continued on at that. (Indeed)
Bulanbulan Sulemani, (Indeed)
Along with Yari Sise, (Indeed)
He sent them forth, (Indeed)
That they should go after horses, (Indeed)
Saying the Manden belonged to him. (Indeed)
Bulanbulan Sulemani, (Indeed)
Along with Yari Sise, (Indeed)
They went on after the horses, (Indeed)
In the land of Dark Jòlòf. (Indeed)
The Dark Jòlòf king fell on the messengers, (Indeed)
And seizing the nine and ninety stallions, (Indeed)
Selected hound dogs one score and ten, (Indeed)
Saying to the Nyani King give them, (Indeed)
Saying he knew Son-Jara for naught (Indeed)
Save a runner of dogs,
Saying he had no reason to doubt that. (That's the truth)

O Garan! (Indeed)
Biribiriba in his hut with his wife, (Indeed)
The bards came up to him singing:

"Khalif Magan Kònatè! (Yes, Fa-Digi)
"Succeeded, the King succeeded! (Indeed)
"The Sorcerer and Sovereignty! (Indeed)
"Who has seen the goat bite a dog?
"O Nare Magan Kònatè!
"Will you not arise?" (Indeed)
Son-Jara transformed himself on the spot,
And turned into a lion, (Indeed)
Saying he was going out after those bards. (Indeed)
His wife grabbed hold and soothed him, (Indeed)
And had him lay back down, (Indeed)
. . . (That's the truth)
. . . (Indeed)
Ah! Kala Jula Sangoyi! (Indeed)
Those are the words the bards said that day: (True)
"O Wizard, (Indeed)
" 'Twas you who sent Bulanbulan Sulemani
"Along with Yari Sise (Indeed)
"That they should go . . . (Indeed)
"After nine and ninety stallions. (Indeed)
"To thirty. (Indeed)
"It was he who plundered the horses, (Indeed)
"And thirty . . . , (Indeed)
"And gave the hound dogs, score and ten, (Indeed)
"Saying we should give you them, (Indeed)
"Since you are but a runner of dogs,
"Saying you have not yet mastered war. (That's the truth)
"O Wizard, a goat bites not a dog!" (That's the truth)

In turn, the warriors swore their fealty: (Indeed)
"Let me the battle-master be!" (Indeed)
Fa-Koli and Tura Magan swore their fealty. (Indeed)
"Let me lead the army!" Fa-Koli
adjured. (That's the truth)

"Let me lead the army!" Tura Magan adjured. (Indeed)
Son-Jara finally spoke, (Indeed)
"'Tis I who will lead the army, (Indeed)
"And go to Dark Jòlòf land." (Indeed)
O Nare Magan Kònatè! (Indeed)
Tura Magan plunged into grief, (Indeed)
And went to the graveyard to dig his grave, (Indeed)

And laid himself down in his grave. (Indeed)
The bards came forth: "O Nare Magan Kònatè, (Indeed)
"If you don't go see Tura Magan, (Indeed)
"Your army will not succeed!" (Indeed)
He sent the bards forth
That they should summon Tura Magan.
And so the bards went forth, (Indeed)
But Tura Magan they could not find. (That's the truth)
Son-Jara came and stood in the graveyard: (Indeed)
"Bugu Turu and Bugu Bò! (Indeed)
"Muke Musa and Muke Dantuman! (Indeed)
"Juru Kèta and Juru Moriba! (Indeed)
"Tunbila the Manden Slave! (Indeed)
"Kalabila, the Manden Slave! (Indeed)
"Sana Fa-Buren, Danka Fa-Buren! (Indeed)
"Dark-Pilgrim and Light-Pilgrim! (Indeed)
"Ah! Bards, (Indeed)
"Let us give the army to Tura Magan, (Indeed)
"To the Slave-of-the-Tomb, Tura Magan, (Indeed)
"O Tura Magan-and-Kanke-jan!" (That's the truth)

Tura Magan spoke out, (Indeed)
"That is the best of all things to my ear!" (Indeed)
To Tura Magan they gave quiver and bow. (Indeed)
Tura Magan advanced to cross the river here, (Indeed)
At the Passage-of-Tura-Magan. (Indeed)
A member of the troop cried out, (Indeed)
"Hey! The war to which we go, (Indeed)
"That war will not be easy! (Indeed)
"Ninety iron drums has the Dark Jòlòf King. (Indeed)
"No drum like this has the Manden, (Indeed)
"Nor balaphone has the Manden. (Indeed)
"There is no such thing in the Manden, (Indeed)
"Save the Jawara patriarch, Sita Fata, (Indeed)
"Save when he puffs out his cheeks, (Indeed)
"Making with them like drum and balaphone,
"To go awaken the Nyani King. (Indeed)
"This battle will not be easy!" (Indeed)
But they drove this agitator off, (Indeed)
Saying better in the bush a frightened brave
Then a loudmouthed agitator. (That's the truth)
He went back across the river, (Indeed)

At the place they call Salakan, (Indeed)
And Ford-of-the-Frightened. (Indeed)
The Ford-of-the-Frightened-Braves. (Indeed)
Tura Magan with battle met. (Indeed)
He slayed that dog-giving king, (Indeed)
Saying he was but running the dogs. (That's the truth)
Tura Magan with army marched on, (Indeed)
He went to slay Nyani Mansa,
Saying he was but running the dogs. (That's the truth)
Tura Magan with the army marched on, (Indeed)
He slayed the Sanumu King,
Saying that he was but running the dogs, (Indeed)
He slayed Ba-dugu King (Indeed)
Saying he was but running the dogs, (Indeed)
And marched on thus through Jòlòf land. (Indeed)
Their name for stone is Jòlòf. (Indeed)
Once there was this king . . . , (Indeed)
The stone there that is red, (Indeed)
The Wòlòf call it Jòlòf. (Indeed)
There once was a king in that country, my father,
Called King of Dark Jòlòfland. (Indeed)
And that is the meaning of this. (That's the truth)
He slayed that Dark Jòlòf King, (Indeed)
Severing his great head at his shoulders, (Indeed)
From whence comes the Wòlòf name, Njòp! (Indeed)
They are Taraweres. (Indeed)
Sane and Mane, (Indeed)
They are Taraweres. (Indeed)
Mayga, they are Taraweres. (Indeed)
Magaraga, they are Taraweres. (Indeed)
Tura Magan-and-Kanke-jan, (Indeed)
He with the army marched on,
To destroy the golden sword and the tall
throne. (That's the truth)
This by the hand of Tura Magan-and-Kanke-jan.
Kirikisa, Spear-of-Access, Spear-of Service! (Indeed)
Ah! Garan! (Indeed)
Let us leave the words right here. (That's the truth,
indeed, it's over now!)

Annotations to the Text

(1) *Nare Magan Kònatè.* Aside from the many and varied praise-names and dialectical pronunciations applied to Son-Jara (Sun-Jata), there are several names by which he is known in Mali. Nare Magan Kònatè is explained as follows. Narena (literally, 'at Nare') is the name of a modern town in Mali, which many people believe was one of the capitals of Son-Jara's empire. There are other towns which claim this prominence—notably Nyani in Guinea—but such variation is to be expected in an oral society. Prefixing the name of one's village of birth or residence (in this case without the suffix *-na*) is a common practice in Mali. Magan is Son-Jara's given name (some say it means 'master'), and Kònatè is the clan name of his father's family.

Another common name follows the Moslem practice in Mali of giving one's first-born son the name of the prophet Muḥammad. Thus, Son-Jara is called Mamadu Kònatè, Mamadu being the Mande pronunciation for the Arabic name. Note here also that the father's surname is added.

Etiological legends based on folk etymologies (see my article on this subject in *Folklore Forum* 9:3/4, 1977) is a favorite combination of genres in Mali and accounts for the name Son-Jara Keyta. Being considered the founder of a clan as well as the empire of Mali entitles this patriarch to a surname of his own. Keyta is explained as being a combination of two Maninka morphemes: *kè,* 'inheritance,' and *ta,* 'to take,' thus, 'He-who-took-(stole)-the-Inheritance,' (implying, 'from his elder brother'). The given name is more complicated, and several variants for its explanation exist. Some lengthen the vowel of Son (Sun), thus Soon (Suun), and claim that it is a contraction of Son-Jara's mother's name Sogolon (Sugulun). Here again we observe a common naming custom in Mali, that of prefixing one's own name with one's mother's name. Others prefer to define Son as 'thief' (*nson*). Jata is almost always considered to mean 'lion.' Thus the full meaning could be 'Soon's Lion/Lion Thief-Who-Took-the-Inheritance.' This folk etymology is generally followed by an etiological legend stating that, because Son-Jara was the second-born son, and yet gained the throne, he usurped Mali from his elder brother; he 'took the inheritance' of his brother. For another legend explaining the thief etymology in the Gambia, see Gordon Innes, *Sunjata* : *Three Mandinka Versions* (London: School of Oriental and African Studies, 1974): pp. 47–48, lines 136–80.

(2) *Subaa-Minè-Subaa,* 'Sorcerer-Seizing-Sorcerer.' Praise-name for Son-Jara, sometimes heard in conjunction with two clan names (Magasubaa and Jarasubaa), which form a rhyming three-pattern. It is an important praise-name for Son-Jara, because it emphasizes his occult power. Many consider the skillful use of magic a necessity for kings to maintain their power.

(4) *Four Mastersingers.* Slightly obscure, this line may be an invocation to the bard's inherited social status as a casted mastersinger. All four casted groups in Mali deal in the occult and thus in secretive and skillful use of language: therefore, four mastersingers. Each caste specializes in the unique economic activity reserved for its well-being. The *jeli* (bard) passes along certain types of verbal information, notably narrative and epic poetry, for remuneration. The *numu* (blacksmith) may specialize in a number of skills associated with metal work and woodcarving. Leather work is sanctioned for the *garangè* (cordwainer), while religious (Islamic) praise-poetry is reserved for the *funè*. Other economic pursuits such as weaving are not casted among Mande peoples, but are casted among neighboring groups such as the Fulani (Peul).

A note must be given on the social status of casted peoples in Mali. Castes are not vertical, as in India, but horizontal. By this image, I mean that Mande castes function more like trade monopolies than pecking-order social classes.

(5) *Kala Jula Sangoyi Mamunaka Jabaatè.* An invocation to a legendary bard of Old Mali. Fa-Digi considers this bard to be the son of the Tarawere hunter Dan Mansa Wulanba (see lines 468ff and the genealogy charts in the appendix). Some people in the Kita area believe that this bard originated the epic of Son-Jara. Some bards describe Kala Jula as a hunting companion to Son-Jara (see, for example, Massa Makan Diabaté, *Kala Jata,* Bamako, Mali: Éditions Populaires, 1970).

(9) *Ben Adam.* First man on earth by Moslem, Jewish, and Christian

traditions. Ben, *bani,* is borrowed from Arabic here as a name. In Arabic, it is actually the plural form of *ibn* (*bin* medially). *Bani Adama,* 'sons of Adam,' is a common epithet for humanity in the Koran.

(10–11) These lines set the scene for the beginning of the narrative. Epic poetry amongst Mande peoples often begins with an etiological, sometimes allegorical, scene-setting legend.

(13) *Biribiriba.* Praise-name for Son-Jara, the meaning of which is obscure.

(16–17) *Fatiyataligara* and *Sokoto.* Description of the land mass of the ancient empire of Mali. Sokoto is a city in modern northern Nigeria and was an important settlement in the nineteenth-century Fulani theocratic empire in that region. Fatiyataligara is obscure, but one assistant considered it the homeland of the Soninke in present-day Mauritania.

(19) *My father.* A term of respect directed to the bard's audience. This stylistic device is employed often by Fa-Digi.

(20) *Republic of Mali.* Note how the bard employs the modern name of the country for the old empire. The word Mali, according to M. Delafosse, *La Langue Mandingue et ses Dialects* (Paris: Paul Geuthner, 1929): Vol. I, p. 9, is derived from the West African ethnic group called Fulani, and is not actually a Mande word. The Manden (Mandin, Manding) is the indigenous term for the original kingdom, now a small portion of Mali and Guinea. (Note that I am using the term Manden for the kingdom and, following J. H. Greenberg, *The Languages of Africa,* Bloomington, Indiana: Indiana University Press, 1966, I use the term Mande to denote the language group.) The first chroniclers of this region were north African Arabs, and they probably acquired the name of the region from Fulani merchants involved in the trans-Saharan trade. Another, perhaps more realistic, explanation for the modern word Mali involves natural sound shifts in the language. The alveolar "nd" shifts to "l" and the terminal vowel denasalizes and raises; thus "Manden" shifts to "Mali."

(21) *Maninka.* Name of Son-Jara's ethnic group, and a Kita regional variant of Manden-ka, 'citizen of/person from the Manden.'

(23–30) Praise-poem symbolizing the conquests of Son-Jara. Note that the names of the three fictitious men slain in the poem form word plays with the stated motivation for the slayings. This type of formulaic expression is common in praise-poetry and can be found in many such poems.

(24–25) *Dankun,* 'border,' literally 'village border.' Description of a normal Mande farming community is necessary to understand this symbol. The cosmologically safest place in Manden worldview is the village (*dugu*), composed of several family compounds (*lulu,* sg. *lu*) around a village square (*bara*). The farther outwards one goes from the core, the more dangerous life becomes, thus increasing the need for occult preparation to face the outside. Passing over the village border (*dankun*), where many sacrifices are performed, one enters the ring of women's vegetable gardens (*na-ko*). Farther out is the toilet ring (*bò-kè-yòrò*), bordered by the men's main cultivation fields (*foro*). This latter ring may be mixed with abandoned fields (*san-gwan*), and on the other side of these outreaches of civilization lies the wilderness (*wula*), the most dangerous of regions, literally and cosmologically. It continues to the fields of the next village.

These lines imply that only strong men with sufficient knowledge of the occult should settle anywhere outside the village border. For the weak, it could spell disaster.

(26–27) *Basa,* 'lizard.' The lizard is considered the property of youth, that is, uncircumcised boys, who are said to practice their first task as a hunter by stalking lizards. The boys cook and eat their catch in a form of communion similar to that of their elders in a communion of heart and liver meat cooked immediately after the kill. These lines imply that if a man takes lizard as his name (or totem?), he takes on the attributes of a weak animal. Note the contrast with the praise-name of the conqueror, *Jata,* 'lion.'

(28–29) These lines carry the same cosmological significance as lines 24–25. See the note above.

(32) *Simbon, Lion-Born-of-the-Cat.* Praise-name for Son-Jara emphasizing his knowledge of hunting and the occult. The latter praise-name is translated here according to one variant folk etymology reported to me by Youssouf Tata Cissé. According to Youssouf, hunters in Mali are said to gain their knowledge of hunting, as well as herbal and occult medicine, by observing the animals of the wilderness (a dangerous business) and passing on their secret knowledge only to apprentices. The valiant hunter (*simbon*) is thus said to have learned his profession from the lion, who himself learned to hunt from his ancestor, the master-hunter cat. *Simbon* is an honorific title for a hunter, which D. T. Niane reports was derived from the Maninka word for hunter's whistle in his, *Soundiata: An Epic of Old Mali* (London: Longman, 1965): note 5, p. 86. For other variant explanations, see Gordon Innes, *Sunjata: Three Mandinka Versions* (London: School of Oriental and African Studies): note 154, p. 106. The variant cited there is *Nyankumolu Khaba la Simbong,* 'Cats on the shoulder Simbong.' Another variant explanation I collected is *Dan-*

kun-ba la wara la Simbon, 'At-the-Great-Bcrder, Simbon-of-the-Bush.'

(34–36) *Stump-in-the-Dark-of-Night.* Praise-name for Son-Jara, emphasizing his ruthlessness, which can strike before the enemy knows it.

(37–41) *Granary-Guard-Dog.* Praise-name for Son-Jara, emphasizing his ruthlessness. Farmers often keep guard dogs to protect their compounds, especially the granary. This guard dog is so ruthless he will bite even members of the compound who are familiar to him.

(42) *Kirikara Watita.* Idiophone representing the rising and falling of the hero's shoulders, symbolizing the arrogance of power. Another assistant reported this praise-line as an epithet used in the Komo Society for a berserk, a ruthless and fearless warrior. The Komo Society is an esoteric cult among the Mande peoples concerned with occult medicine.

(43) *Adversity's-True-Place.* Praise-name for Son-Jata, emphasizing his ruthlessness.

(44) The Maninka line is vague and could mean that the reason for a man's and a woman's existence, or their ability to reason and think, are not the same.

(46–48) *Nine and ten Adams.* The reference is obscure. Possibly a metaphor for the races of humanity, the nine Adams might symbolize the creation of other heavenly creatures, such as jinns and angels (e.g., "the company of heaven").

(49) *Bènba.* Name of the Bard's naamusayer. The naamusayer, often the bard's apprentice, is responsible for giving the bard encouragement. His responses can direct the course of the narrative to some degree. An excited response can cause the bard to develop an idea, while a weak response can discourage him. I witnessed a naamusayer go to sleep on his bard one night and begin to snore, but he never missed a response!

(54) *Iblis.* Arabic name of God's most beloved Angel. According to the Islamic faith, he refused to bow down before Adam and was transformed into the *shaydan,* 'satan,' and cast out of heaven.

(64) *Sibiri,* 'hand span.' A traditional measurement which is the length of the distance between the middle finger and the outstretched thumb, used in Mali for measuring such items as cloth and rope. Its counterpart is the *nogon,* 'cubit,' measuring the distance between elbow and middle finger. Variation of length occurs since not all people have the same measurements.

(66) Etiological explanation of how the power of satan came to be established. Because of his greed, he demands repayment for his years of service. God creates wealth (line 80) and gives it to satan,

thereby unleashing its misuse upon humanity through the power of the devil.

(72) *Trumpet blows.* In Moslem (as in Christian) theology, the angel Jilbril (Gabriel) will blow the horn announcing the end of time. This traditional motif will be recognized as Motif A 1093: end of world announced by trumpet, in Stith Thompson, *Motif Index of Folk-Literature* (Bloomington, Indiana: Indiana University Press, 1966). All motifs cited in the text are from Thompson's index.

(75–97) Parts of a poem sometimes get "lost in translation." This passage serves as a good example of that problem. Here the bard plays on the verb root *fili,* 'to throw/be mistaken/fail to recognize.' His skillful use of this verb with prefixes and suffixes yields several words and phrases such as *nòfili,* 'to lead astray' in line 73 and *filiman-kan,* 'the voice of sin/transgression' in line 82.

The obscurity of this passage also requires explanation. From lines 56 to 82, the characters of the narrative speak. Then the bard comments on the nature of the Voice of Transgression from lines 83 to 88, explaining that if one has wealth, one will ignore one's kinsmen. If one has no wealth, one's kinsmen will ignore him. Lines 90 through 96 are the Voice of Transgression itself metaphorically speaking to its disciples, the sinners. In three couplets, the Voice of Transgression explains that if a person does not use his wealth for others, his downfall is secured. In line 97 the bard again comments, invoking God's protection for the weak from the wealthy.

(103) *Jinn.* A spirit in Moslem theology that is invisible to human beings, though some live in communities on the earth. Some jinns are beneficial to humanity—the English words genie and genius derive from this Arabic word—and others are hostile. Many people in Mali believe that some cohabit with humans to produce superheroes like Fa-Koli, one of Son-Jara's generals. In Mande folklore, jinns are often thought to live in fetishes and are consulted for advice and guidance.

(106) *Morality.* Other possible translations for *maluya* are 'conscience,' 'decency,' and 'shame.'

(115–17) *Dignity.* According to Moslem theology, human beings were the most important of God's creatures, so all of heaven's company was told to bow down before Adam (see note for line 54). Satan's refusal caused him to be cast from heaven. Whereas the Christian concept of original sin tends to place humanity at the bottom of the cosmological pecking order, Islam puts us at the top. A confirmation of this belief may be observed in the tenet that God forgave Adam for the first sin. The Moslem messiah, *mahdi,* does not function as the reconciler of the sin of Adam. Another confirmation of this belief may be observed in lines 116–20, where God creates the most important of his creations, Muḥammad the Prophet, as a human, not as a jinn or angel.

(121) *Filardi Samawaati.* Obscure passage. Could be the Maninka pronunciation for the Arabic *fi 'l-ardi wa samāwāti,* 'on earth and in heaven.' Line 122 below would seem to confirm this possibility.

(123) Line unclear on tape. Ellipses will be used throughout the text to indicate unintelligibility.

(130) *India.* The term in Maninka, *Hindi,* may simply mean 'the East.' See lines 133–34 below.

(140–44) The bard metaphorically describes an eclipse of the moon by the sun. The phrase concerning the cat is commonly recited by youths during such an eclipse.

(147–52) Reference to Islamic theology. Omitting the episode of Adam and Eve in the Garden, the bard resumes his narrative when the pair have been cast out of paradise. In Moslem belief, God cast them out separately and caused them to seek after each other for forty days and forty nights. Eventually Adam sees Eve before she sees him, thus ordaining masculine initiative in seeking a spouse. Since this narrative still exists in the oral tradition, variants exist. Some say Adam found Eve in Lebanon, while others, including Fa-Digi, claim that Eve was found atop Mount Arfa (Arafan). The mountain is in Mecca and plays a role in Moslem pilgrimage (*ḥājj*) ceremonies.

(155–56) In other words, they had forty sets of twins, a boy and a girl each time. Twins could not marry each other, but were permitted to intermarry with their siblings, thus beginning the world's population.

(164) *Masusu* and *Masasa.* Obscure place names. The Bible calls the descendants of Japheth 'the Coastal Peoples' (Gen. 10:5), which would agree with line 163. Masusu and Masasa may be the same as the Bible's Mesha, (Gen. 10:30), but this was the home of Shem, not Japheth. Kalilou Tèra recounted a legend that credits Alexander the Great (Julu Kara Nayini) for building a great range of mountains (the Himalayas?) to keep out these people, who were considered barbaric. The suggestion is that these are the yellow races, which is confirmed by Moslem tradition. They complete the three-patterned descendants of Noah (See notes for lines 165–67).

(165) *Ham.* Note that Fa-Digi credits Ham as the ancestor of the black race, although not for the pejorative reasons suggested by Motif A 1614.1, Negroes as curse on Ham for laughing at Noah's nakedness.

(169) *Kirikisa.* Term obscure to all the assistants. *Spear-of-Acceṣs, Spear-*

of-Service. Praise-name for Son-Jara implying a force for the good of humanity.

(171) *Dònba month*. This word does not appear to be Arabic in origin. The Prophet's birthday (*Mawlīd*) is celebrated on the twelfth day of the month of *Shawwal*.

(173) *Bilāl bin Rabaḥ*, sometimes called Ibn Ḥamāma after his mother, is referred to in Mande as Jòn Bilali, 'Servant/Slave Bilali.' One of the bards from whom I collected, Ban Sumana Sisòkò, explained the name *jòn* as a religious one, with the same connotation as the Arabic ʿabd al-Lāh (ʿAbdallāh), 'slave/servant of God.' Islamic historical writings do describe Bilāl as a slave, first of Umayya bin Khalaf (an unbeliever whom Bilāl later slew in battle) and then of Abū Bakr (the Prophet Muḥammad's father-in-law and the first convert of Islam). Whether genealogical claims of kinship between the Mande peoples and Bilāl are historical or merely legendary is of little consequence to folk belief. Many African Moslems claim kinship to the Prophet or to those close to him, because of the Islamic belief that *barakah*, 'grace/power,' can be inherited from Muḥammad's descendants or intimates. The Mande peoples probably claim kinship to Bilāl, because he is described as being of Ethiopian (African?) origin. The belief is supported by the Black Moslem movement in America. In late 1975 the name of the Black Moslem newspaper *Muhammad Speaks* was changed to the *Bilalian News*.

Bilāl's tomb is still standing in Damascus (see Philip K. Hitti, *History of the Arabs*, (London: Macmillan, 1967, note 1, page 106). He is considered the first *mu'aḍḍin (mu'aẓẓin)* or prayer-caller and the second convert to Islam. He is said to have been the Prophet's mace-bearer (*ʿanaza*), steward (*khazin*), and personal servant and adjutant. He accompanied Muḥammad on his holy wars (*jiḥad*), and continued in service as a warrior in Syria after the death of the Prophet. As a Companion or Disciple (*al-Saḥābī, al-Saḥīb*), of Muḥammad, some 44 of the Islamic Traditions (*aḥādith*), which are short, legendary stories and treatises concerning the deeds and teaching of the Messenger of God, are attributed to Bilāl. For a more detailed description of the life and accomplishments of Bilāl bin Rabaḥ, and for a bibliography of further references, see W. 'Arafat's article in *The Encyclopaedia of Islam: New Edition* (London: Luzac & Co., 1960): vol. vi, p. 1215.

Samuda. Maninka pronunciation of *Thamūda*, name of a clan and the city of its origin in Arabia. Later, when Muḥammad proclaimed his prophecy, this clan opposed him. A Moslem legend states that once Muḥammad came to water his camel at a well the Thamūda were using. A confrontation followed and the Thamūda killed the Prophet's camel. Later they were defeated by the Prophet's forces.

(176–81) Note that these men are the legendary ancestors of the noble clans (*hòròn*) of old Mali.

(184) *Maraka* (possibly *Mara-ka,* 'people of Mara'). Maninka word for the Soninke (Sarakole) ethnic group. They were the last rulers of Ghana (Wagadugu). The Maraka live in present-day Mali near Segu.

(185) *Wagadugu,* 'Land of the Waga.' Also known as Ghana (Gāna) in Arabic chronicles, the empire of Gāna, which reached its zenith under the Soninke rulers in the ninth and tenth centuries, was the first of the three great empires of West Africa during the Middle Ages. The other two were Mali and Songhoy. This Wagadugu, which was located mostly in what is today Mauritania, must not be confused with the name of the modern capital city of Upper Volta. Nor should the empire of Gāna be confused with the modern West African state of Ghana.

(186–94) Listing of Bamana and Maninka surnames, except for Fulani and Jawara, which are names for ethnic groups.

(195) The allusion is to the legend of the snake of Wagadugu, subject of a Soninke epic. According to the variant given by one of my assistants, the great snake of Koumbi Saleh, capital of Wagadugu, received the annual sacrifice of a virgin. One year the chosen girl was spared, because the snake, who dwelt in a pit, was killed by the girl's lover. The man had to cut off its head nine times in order to kill it, but before it died, the snake cursed the land, causing a drought of nine years, nine months, and nine days. Thus, the people of this great empire had to disperse to other areas. The belief in this dispersion is the basis for many modern clan and ethnic etiological claims.

(197) *Damangile.* Ancestor of the Jawara ethnic group. Damangile (Daman N'Guilé) is said to have been a giant, and his tomb measures some 20 to 25 feet long. For a thorough ethnology of the Jawara, see G. Boyer, *Un Peuple de l'Ouest Soudanais: les Diawara* (Dakar, Senegal: Institut Français d'Afrique Noire, 1953): pp. 123 and plates. For a résumé of the legend of Damangile, see especially pp. 21–22 and Plate I, Figure 3.

(198) *Nyenemba Nyarè.* Ancestor of the Nyarè clan of the Manden. The modern capital of Mali, Bamako, is said to have been a Nyarè settlement originally, and this clan lives there in great numbers.

(199) *Kingi.* A traditional region located in the western part of modern Mali, bordering Mauritania. The city of Nyoro du Sahel is the principal settlement of this region.

(200) *Bambagile.* Probably the modern village of Bambagèdè, about 40 kms. east of Nyoro du Sahel.

(204) *Jala.* Probably the modern village of Jara, about 30 kms. west of Nyoro du Sahel.

(205) *Mount Siman and Mount Wala.* Small mountains presumably found in the area around Jara and Bambagèdè.

(207) *Prince Burama.* Ancestor of the Tunkara clan, his title *Farin* is a Soninke title. Burama is the Maninka pronunciation of the Arabic name Ibrāhīm (Abraham).

(208) *Mèma.* Often mentioned in Mande folklore, the exact site of Mèma is debated. Some bards equate it with the modern village of Nèma in Mauritania, but other bards deny the claim. If it existed, it was probably located in the area around Mopti and Djenné, on the west bank of the Niger River. Son-Jara will later spend his exile in this country.

(210) *Prince Burama.* Note that this Prince Burama is the son of the Prince Burama in line 207.

(215) *Kulun.* Location of this village is obscure. Because of the other villages mentioned, it must be somewhere between Nyoro and Kita.

(217) *Bangasi.* This village is about 40 kms. east of Kita, some 10 kms. north of the railroad line.

(218) *Mount Genu.* This mountain is located in the Kita region and is also called Mount Kita.

(220) *Kuduguni.* Whether this village exists now is not clear. Folk etymologies suggested for its meaning were 'village of the yam' and 'the little hidden thing.'

(226) *Kita.* Somewhat over 150 kms. west of Bamako, Kita is on the railroad line from Bamako to Dakar. Note that this variant was recited by a Kita bard.

(230) *Warlord,* etc. Praise-name for Son-Jara, emphasizing his ruthlessness. The final term, *fara,* 'a pile of stone' is translated conjecturally.

(238) *Ki-Kè-Bugu,* 'Farming Hamlet.' In Maninka village geography (see note for lines 24–25 above), a family normally lives in the *lu,* 'compound,' but goes out of the village to work in the fields (*foro*). During the planting and harvest seasons, the farmer may construct a temporary lean-to or hut (*bugu*) in the midst of the fields. Often several farmers construct their huts together, and their collection of huts can become the nucleus of a new village.

(240) *Manden Kiri-kòròni.* This village is said to have been the first village in the Manden. The traditional regions of Kiri and Du—we shall see much of Du later—are said to be the oldest in Mali.

(246) *Dankò*. Conjectural transcription. According to one assistant, the modern name of this clan is Danfaga. Another assistant transcribed Dabò, another surname.

(248) *Kòròlen,* etc. These men are sons of the same father but different mothers (*fa-denlu*). Fabu, born of Kòròlen, and Fabu, born of Sòkòna, prefix their names with their mother's name for clarity. This is a common practice in Mali.

(249) *Dugunò*. A clan family of bards.

(250) As one would expect in an oral society, the genealogy in this text is the opinion of the bard and not a universally accepted line of descent. The descendants which follow (to line 256) are obscure to my assistants. Fata Magan, the Handsome is Son-Jara's father.

(258) *Kakama*. This area is said to have been the place where Fata Magan kept his fields. It was located in Bintanya Kamalen.

(259) *Bintanya Kamalen*. One of the traditional designations for the Manden heartland. This small region is located partly in Mali and partly in Guinea. In Mali the famous village of Kaaba (Kangaba) is the center of this region and, according to many, of the entire Mande-speaking world.

(269–70) Note that the number 33 is a pattern-number and not a literal mathematical figure. The bard actually lists 35 clans in lines 271–76.

(269) *Tun-tan-mògò,* 'noble clans.' A difficult word to translate, this word may be idiosyncratic to Fa-Digi. After consultation with assistants, we agreed to translate *tun-tan-mògò* as 'noble clan,' and *tun-tan-jòn* (line 271) as 'warrior.' For a good discussion on Bambara associations (*tun*), see Claude Meillassoux's *Urbanization of an African Community: Voluntary Associations in Bamako* (Seattle: University of Washington Press, 1968), especially pp. 49–54.

(272) *Agents*. This term, *jabi-fin-jòn* is translated conjecturally. One assistant described such people as spies.

(273) *Mamuru*. Often included in this list, the assistants did not know who Mamuru was. His descendants are listed on lines 277–81 below.

(274) *Mori,* 'holy-man.' Not only a practitioner of Islamic ritual, the Mande *mori* is said to deal in the occult to some extent. An oft-mentioned *mori* curse is barrenness among rival co-wives. Although the list differs from region to region, my assistants could name several clans specializing in this profession: Sise, Ture, Berete, Tunkara, Jane, and Sila.

(275) *Siya mògò,* 'families that came later.' This line alludes to a Mande tradition which deals with land tenure. The bards explain, using the stylistic formula of listing, that some clans were the original inhab-

itants of the Manden. Among these families, the *bula,* 'original families,' are listed Kamisòkò, Bagayògò, Sisòkò and Dunbiya. The *siya mògò* (*dunan,* 'stranger' is used in Bamana) are explained as clans which arrived in the Manden at a much later period in history. These clans, among them, Tarawele, Jaara, Kònatè, and Keyta, are said to have been conquering warrior clans. Modern Maninka and Bamana village political structure is often organized around this folk belief. A political chief, *dugu-tigi,* is consulted on matters of state, while a ritual chief, *dugu-kolo-tigi,* is consulted in matters of land and religious ceremonies concerning fertility. In many places, though apparently not everywhere, the *dugu-kolo-tigi* is from a *bula* family and the *dugu-tigi* is a *dunan*. Because the *dugu-kolo-tigi* is the descendant of the family considered the first to settle a region, it is also possible for a *dunan* to be a ritual chief.

(276) *Pariah.* Deformed people, or those with epilepsy, are considered by many to be possessed of special occult power (*nyama*). Presumably such a person would be of benefit because of his/her power.

(277–81 and 282–88) The bard lists the names of the patriarchs of the clans or clan branches he mentioned above.

(287) *Fodele, the Tall* was said to be a Tunkara.

(290) *Tariku,* 'chronicle.' From the Arabic word *ta'rikh,* this form of historical narrative is unique in Africa in that it is written down. It was common for some families in several parts of Africa, especially those influenced by Islam, to record their family histories. I heard of this practice in both Mali and Somalia. Some of these books, I was told, are several generations old, having been passed along in each generation to a family historian.

(293) *Quraysh* and *Hāshim.* In Arab tradition, the Quraysh are the descendants of the Prophet Ibrāhīm (Abraham) through his maidservant Hajar (Hagar). Moslems consider Hajar's son Isma<u>ʕ</u>il (Ishmael) to be patriarch of the Arabs, while his younger half-brother Isḥāq (Isaac) is considered to be patriarch of the Jews. The Hāshim are the branch of the Quraysh from which the Prophet Muḥammad descended. See Appendix for Fa-Digi's version of these genealogies.

(294) In Arab tradition, Hāshim, for whom the clan is named, was the father of ʕabd al-Muṭṭalib.

(297) *Fatima Bint.* The Prophet Muḥammad's favorite daughter. Her name Bint (Binta), which is a common Mande name today, is from the feminine form of the Arabic word *ibn* (see the note for line 9 above). The woman's full title in Arabic is *Fāṭimah bintu 'r-Rasūlū 'l-Lāhi,* 'Fāṭimah, Daughter of the Messenger of God.'

(300–303) *Al-Ḥasan* and *al-Ḥusayn.* The twin sons of Fāṭimah and ʕali, fourth Khalif and first Imām of Islam. ʕali was also the Prophet's patrilineal first cousin.

The Prophet's grandsons were given honorific titles, which their descendants retained. Al-Ḥasan was called Sharīf, 'noble,' and al-Ḥusayn took the title Sayyid, 'lord.' (See Hitti, op. cit., n. 8, p. 440).

(304) *Abulayi*. Maninka pronunciation of the Arabic name ʕabd al-Lāhi ('Abdallāhi). At this point in the genealogy, the bard deviates from the traditional records of the Prophet's family genealogy. For this reason, the Maninka form of the name is maintained in the text.

(305–09) *Tarawere*. Etiological legend based on one of several variant folk etymologies for this name. Here, Abulayi is said to have had two pairs of eyes, one in the front of his head and one in the back (perhaps symbolic of a seer or diviner). *Ta ra wa ra* is claimed to be the Arabic form for 'he sees and sees.' Actually, the Maninka translation is closer to the Arabic for 'she sees and sees,' *tara wa tara* ('he sees and sees' is *yara wa yara*). For a broader discussion of this and other surname legends, see my article, "Etiological Legends Based on Folk Etymologies of Manding Surnames," *Folklore Forum* 9:3/4 (Bloomington, Indiana: Forum Society, 1976): 107–14.

(312) *Kayibara*. Place name, presumably in Arabia. I have been unable to find the referent to this Maninka form, but this name is used by others bards and is probably used here for the war (battle?) in which Muḥammad rose to power over the Infidels.

(313) *Remained*. Euphemism for death.

(322–24) *One-Who-Enters,* etc. Praise-names for the Tarawere clan, alluding to obscure legends. The last name, Tura Magan-and-Kankejan is a double or conjoined praise-name for the son of Dan Mansa Wulandin (line 320). Tura Magan later becomes one of Son-Jara's generals and conquers the Gambia for the empire.

(325ff.) Having traced Son-Jara's paternal line back to its origins in Arabia, the bard now turns to the maternal line. As his paternal inheritance contains the power (*barakah*) of Islam, so his maternal inheritance will contain the power of the occult (*nyama*) which he needs in order to overcome his enemies and become king.

The episodes of the Buffalo-Woman and the two Tarawere hunters is rich in overtone. Not only is it a part of the narrative and legend of Son-Jara's maternal line, but it is also a social commentary concerning the nature of respect, responsibility, and affection between members of a family and of society at large.

(326) *Jara, Jata*. Clan name equated with Kòndè (Kònè, Kòntè, Mariko).

Some Mande surnames have regional variants, which do not appear to be linguistic variants, although linguistic variation also occurs. The reason for this type of variation remains obscure. *Sankarandin*. River in Guinea, the Sankaran (*din* is a diminutive) is said to flow through the ancient region of Du (see note for line 240). Note that this bard often uses Sankaran and Du interchangeably to mean the region.

(334) *Dugu-mògòlu-nya-mògò,* 'Leader-of-the-People.' The local title of the ruler of Du according to legend. This title, in variant form, is common to many versions of this epic. For a similar title, see the note for line 207.

(336) *Flesh-and-Blood-Sister*. The translation here is liberal; *ba-kilinma-musu* literally means 'sister-by-the-same-mother[-and-father].' The phrase is an affectionate (and thus often honorific) epithet for a full sister (*ba-den-musu*). Because of the affectionate overtones of this word, it is sometimes used between half siblings (*fa-denlu*) to diminish the rivalry traditional to their relationship. For more about *ba-den* and *fa-den,* see the note for lines 356–59. *Du Kamisa,* 'Kamisa of Du (Do).' This woman, who later becomes the Buffalo-Woman, is considered to have been a great sorceress. From her, Son-Jara's mother will inherit her occult powers, and thus will his sister inherit them. Son-Jara will therefore be surrounded with great occult power. See also the note for lines 325ff.

(339ff.) These lines reveal that Leader-of-the-People has given his son to his sister Du Kamisa to rear. This is an allusion to a common practice in Mali today. If a man has a barren sister, it is customary for one of his sons to be reared in her household. The father retains his responsibility for his son, who retains his father's surname, but the social arrangement permits the sister to enjoy motherhood as a foster mother. I was told that a man may give one of his children to his sister to rear even when she has children of her own. Family ties are strengthened by this practice, which may account for its similar use among co-wives. By "swapping" children, co-wife rivalry can sometimes be diminished.

(341) *Kun-sii-kunan,* 'birth-hair'; literally, 'bitter hair.' Allusion to the Islamic name ceremony, which occurs on the child's eighth day and involves shaving his hair.

(343) *Ko, "Sini Ku."* 'She said, "A thing for tomorrow." ' An alternative translation for lines 342 and 343 could be:

> And put it in a calabash
> Called "The Thing for Tomorrow."

(350) *Swaddling cloth.* A special cloth used to tie a child to its mother's back for transporting. Swaddling cloths are easily recognizable from the traditional patterns embroidered on them, but the cloth itself is often hidden from view by the mother's shawl.

(356–59) Allusion to the ceremony which some kings perform at the beginning of their reigns. The divination and ceremony differ from place to place but often involve the *se* (shea, karité) tree, whose name puns with *se* (power). A part of the ceremony common to the Wasulu area of Mali was described by Borama Soumaouro. In the dark of night, the new king must strip naked and go into the forest. There he sacrifices a horse-head kola nut and climbs into a shea tree, where he shouts, "*Se bè Ne bulu,*" " 'Power/shea-butter is in my hands/possession!' " When he descends from the tree, he must reenter the town without being seen.

In general, a Mande sacrifice is usually a metaphorical ceremony. The bull's black color symbolizes the earth, domain of the dead ancestors. In divining it is a negative symbol, and is represented by a downward-facing token (kola half, cowrie, groundnut shell, etc.). The bull's white color symbolizes the sky, domain of the spiritual world whose forces lead man to adventure and perhaps accomplishment, albeit frought with danger. In divining, this symbol can be interpreted negatively or positively depending on the tradition followed by the diviner. Bearing both colors by the bull symbolizes a balance between the forces of heaven and earth, and thus stability in the future reign of the king.

For reasons not clarified by the bard, the old woman who raised the king and who is not an outsider (*kò-kan-mògò*) is excluded from the ceremony. Her exclusion from this sacrificial ceremony is symbolic of her exclusion from the family. Her resulting anger upsets the very balance of the cosmos the king is seeking in his sacrifice of the bull. His anger is thus unleashed against his aunt, which ironically upsets further the balance he seeks. The mark of a Mande hero is his ability to survive violation of social sanction and tabu. This king is no hero, for he is quite unable to control the results of the imbalance in the form of the Buffalo-Woman. This monster of the occult world ravages the land and upsets the balance of life in a manner which would prove the end of the clan. Such sorcery requires hunter-heroes to counteract the forces and reestablish the order, for the wilderness and its danger and secretive knowledge are their domain. These hunters correct the imbalance by reestablishing the responsibility of youth to respect and love their elders. Generosity succeeds where weapons fail, for it was not weapons but a relationship which was violated in the first place. Herein we observe one of the many contemporary didactic functions of the epic of Son-Jara.

The cosmological terms in Mande for balance (*ba-denya*) and chaos (*fa-denya*), which also mean 'cooperation' versus 'rivalry,' are derived from traditional role playing in the extended family. Half siblings (*fa-den,* 'father's child') are expected to fight for their father's inheritance and exercise rivalry. Full siblings (*ba-den,* 'mother's child') are expected to cooperate with each other and express affection. The bound morpheme {-YA} here shifts these nouns to a different class. On a cosmological scale *ba-denya* and *fa-denya* are said to compete for control, and it is to the hunter that villagers often turn to reestablish balance.

(361) In theory, one must defer to all one's elders or one's spouse's elders (according to his/her family status). Therefore, living near an elder could limit one's personal freedom. There may be other reasons why the aunt chose to live apart, perhaps having to do with the status roles of younger sisters, about which I am unacquainted.

(362) *A ni wura,* 'you and the bush.' The bard begins these praise lines with a greeting. This form of greeting is formulaic and could be designated thus: 'you and X.' Compare these other greetings common in Mande society:

> *I ni cè,* 'you and the work' (also 'thank you')
> *I ni sugu,* 'you and the market' (said to a woman on her way to the market)
> *I ni gwa,* 'you and the kitchen' (said to a woman who has prepared a meal for you)
> *I ni sògòma/tilen/wula/su,* 'you and the morning/day/evening/night' ('good morning/day/evening/night')

(368) *Great-Host-Slaying-Stranger.* Praise-name for Son-Jara emphasizing his ruthlessness. Any hero who violates the sanction of honoring one's host and survives the resulting cosmological imbalance is protected by the occult and gains even more protection from the violation of social norms.

(369) *Lòn,* 'to know.' Often associated with the occult, this verb may be used metaphorically in Mande. To know is to control; thus, one who has too much knowledge about a person is potentially threatening to that person.

(403) *Family sacrifice.* See lines 356–59 above.

(409) *Lamb-skin.* At a Moslem name-giving ceremony in many places in Mali (see the note for line 341 above) a lamb is sacrificed, and the skin is given to the paternal aunt. The skin symbolizes the relation-

ship of a nephew to his aunt, for whom there is a specific term (*tènè* or *tana*).

(418) *Slashed off breasts* suggest motif Q 451.9. Punishment: woman's breasts cut off. This motif is frequently used in Mande folklore (see also line 2724), and powerfully symbolizes the nullification of a woman as a social person. Breasts represent a woman's primary social activity and symbolize her links to a social group. They are an important metaphor for affection and love.

Magasi. Idiophone for the sound of slashing.

(442–46) Proverb. If one deceives a person into buying an underfed horse, then one must compensate by providing a means for cutting grass for it. The sense here is that Leader-of-the-People's bad treatment of his aunt (like selling a skinny horse) must be compensated for (grass cutter). The compensation becomes manifest in revenge.

(459) *Du ka Ginda,* 'The *Ginda* of Du.' Praise-name for the buffalo. Its meaning is obscure.

(474) *Kola*. Coming in two colors (red and white) and in many sizes, this nut is chewed throughout West Africa for its stimulant effects, as it contains caffeine. The Kola nut plays an important role in Mande social life, and is used in many social situations including greeting. Kola is also used extensively as a sacrifice, and it is to this function that the bard refers here.

(475ff.) The act of sacrificing is often preceded by divination, which helps determine the nature of the problem and its remedy. In this case, the hunters will use groundnuts (peanuts) for the divination process.

(476) It is understood by the Mande audience that the hunters have gone to the jinn to obtain the means and occult preparation for killing the buffalo.

(477) *Tiningbè Magan*. Name of the jinn. The possible meaning of the first name is obscure, although *gbè* is most likely the adjective 'white/clear/light/pale.'

(479ff.) These lines recited by one of the hunters are an incantation to summon the jinn to come forth. Lines 479 (which puns with the word for salamander) and 480 suggest an image of a round-headed monster with a pale face, flaky from leprous sores.

(481) *Nyagatè*. A Soninke surname, its usage here is obscure.

(491–94) The jinn summoned, the hunter casts the groundnut shell halves. Casting one up (toward the sky) and one down (toward the ancestors), symbolizing a balance in the cosmos, is apparently interpreted as static by the younger brother (see note for lines 356-59), who becomes angry and wants to kill the jinn. Oral transmission often results in variant forms of interpretation. A positive interpretation of the one-up, one-down sign can be found in Charles S. Bird, et al., *The Songs of Seydou Camara: Vol. I. Kambili* (Bloomington, Indiana: African Studies Center at Indiana University, 1974): n. 132, p. 117.

(495–501) *Su-dòn-fòli,* 'dirge.' This dirge is said to have been sung at Son-Jara's funeral. Some bards add a third line, thus:

> Min yena kèlè kè, i ka kèlè kè!
> He who would do battle, let him do battle!

One assistant reported that the dirge celebrates the three honorable professions of a freeman in the Manden.

(505) This *Nyani*—and there were several different *Nyanis* in Old Mali—is said to have been located on the Sankaran River (see note for line 326), just across the Mali-Guinea border. The word can be glossed as 'misery,' but it may be a homophone. Son-Jara's praise-name Nyani Mansa is sometimes explained as punning with this meaning and that of 'King of Nyani.'

(515) *Aramuri.* This type of sand divination is cast on the back of a Koranic board (*walan*), a piece of wood measuring about eight inches by two to four feet upon which children learn to write Koranic scriptures.

(522–23) The sacrifice metaphor involved here (see note for lines 356–59) is obscure. The function of the sacrifice, however, is to hex the food and bring the old woman under the power of the hunters by getting her to eat it.

(529–32) This sequence may have been symbolized by the position of the groundnut shell halves in the divination by the jinn (see notes for lines 491–94). One up (hunters in bush, buffalo in town) and one down (hunters in town, buffalo in bush) equals static action.

(537) Laughing often accompanies extreme nervousness, and may thus be considered a traditional gesture among the Manden. The old woman sees what is happening to her and is fearful at first. The hunters finally bring her under their power by a show of respect and generosity.

(550ff.) The old woman gives up the secret of her vulnerability not only because the offense against her has been revenged but also because she realizes her time has come. She does not have the requisite power to defeat the brothers.

(554–55) In other words, the old woman grew so fat from eating and drinking that the folds of fat in her belly swelled up and popped out.

(560) *Genda-Kala,* 'spindle.' Tool used for spinning cotton and woolen fibers into thread. A typical Mande spindle is made of a thin stick about eight inches long, piercing a decorated, baked clay ball about one-and-a-half inches in diameter. This tool will be used as an occult weapon to kill the buffalo, for it contains no iron. The buffalo cannot be wounded by metal weapons.

(564) *New calabashes* are used in many ceremonies and may be symbolic of the womb.

(565) The traditional gesture of linking little fingers for oath swearing is a common practice in West Africa.

(579) *Cobra,* and the following creatures are invoked to strike down any oath swearer who breaks his/her word.

(583) *Baobab* and other trees are considered sacred, some for specific purposes.

(585) *The deer fly* bites fiercely, thus his inclusion in the list.

(586) *The datu leaf* (it may be a variety of wood sorrel) is used in the preparation of sauce. The stink it gives off is similar to putrifying flesh and is here symbolic of the smell of death.

(596ff.) The magic flight with helpful objects suggests motif D 672. Obstacle flight. Fugitives throw objects behind them which magically become obstacles in pursuer's path (Thompson, 1966).

(606) *Tun,* 'anthill'; literally 'termite hill.' The soil from these giant mounds possesses special chemical characteristics and is mixed with mud and straw in the manufacture of bricks in some parts of Africa.

(612ff.) *Dibi,* 'shade/shadow/obscurity/invisibility.' The shade discussed here is an occult invisibility, the results of an occult preparation explained by the Buffalo-Woman. Such conjuring can be directed against specific persons to whom and perhaps only to whom the conjurer will appear invisible. The spell may not make the hunter invisible to all; it may only make the buffalo unable to see the hunter.

(613) In other words, 'Even in our own time.'

(639ff.) The buffalo begins to pursue the hunters over a vast stretch of land. The bard lists the kingdoms through which the flight occurs, and alludes to etiological legends concerning their origins. It is not unlikely that the town names have some metaphorical value, but I have not found a satisfying exegesis.

(643) *Bèmbè.* Place name, obscure to all the assistants.

(644) *Tala Mansa Kòngò,* 'Rescurer-King-of-the-Wilderness' (and elsewhere Tali Mansa Kòngò, 'Bee-King-of-the-Wilderness'). Ancestor of the blacksmith clan of Kamisòkò, this king is said to have been a great wizard. Some say his totem is the bee, thus the one interpreta-

tion of his praise-name. Tala Mansa Kòngò was king of Kirina, about 50 kms. southwest of Bamako.

(645ff.) Praise-poem addressed to Tala Mansa Kòngò and the Kamisòkò clan. *Kiri*. One of the ancient regions of old Mali, north of the Manden and south of Du (Do). See note for line 240. Kirina, literally 'at Kiri' is one of Kiri's principal towns.

(648) *Tèrè Kunba* and *Kaya*. Slightly obscure, but probably place names for early Kamisòkò settlements. Kaya, I was told, is the traditional name for the region around the town of Kita.

(649) *Nyani River* and *Maramu River*. Used as Kamisòkò praises because they have clan settlements there, the locations of these rivers were obscure to the assistants.

(650) Obscure line, but it may be a symbolic reference to the two branches of the Kamisòkò: the warrior branch (the bow) and the blacksmith branch (the hammer).

(651) *Kaarta*. Name of a traditional region and kingdom (from mid seventh to mid nineteenth centuries) of Bamana people. This region lies from the border with Mauritania around the cities of Nioro du Sahel and Nara, south to the area just north of Kita and east to the Niger River.

(652) *Magasa*. Regional variant of the surname Kamisòkò, or possibly a lineage or subclan. See the note for line 326.

(653) *Fa-Koli Dumbiya*. Nephew of Sumamuru, this warrior later deserts his uncle to become one of Son-Jara's generals. The breach is especially significant because Fa-Koli is a sister's son to Sumamuru, and this relationship is one of *ba-denya* and affection (see note for lines 356–59). Fa-Koli is considered in these lines the ancestor of all the *bula* clans (see the note for line 275), the oldest of which is considered to be Dumbiya; the other clans are said to be branches of this one. It should be pointed out, however, that this role for Fa-Koli and his role in the epic is a telescoped anachronism. The story takes place well after the establishment of the *bula* families.

(668ff.) Praise-poem to the Kòndè (Jara) clan, most of which is obscure. The poem emphasizes the ruthlessness of Kòndè heroes, as in line 675, which praises the violation of a tabu. If a Mande hero can violate a tabu (here killing a kinsman) and survive the resulting release of occult power (*nyama*), then he may gain control over that power (line 677).

(671) *Fa-Kanda*. Obscure phrase, probably a praise-name for a Kòndè ancestor. The words may be glossed as 'birthright/inheritance,' *fa* being the word for father and *kanda* being that spiritual and mystical power inherited from the lineage.

(684) *Garabaya and Kaya.* Obscure place names. For data on Kaya, see the note for line 648.

(688ff.) Note the shift in the praise-poem from the Kòndè clan to Son-Jara.

(698) *Biri-biri-biri.* Idiophone for the sound of heaviness. The reduplication is a common intensifier and can denote repeated events.

(699) *Shea-butter tree.* See the note for lines 356–59.

(720) *Pan.* Idiophone, either for the sound of the spindle leaving the bow (e.g. "twang"), or for the sound of it piercing the buffalo's hide (e.g. "thppp").

(722–28) The Buffalo-Woman cries her last words in praise-proverb mode, the last four lines of which are a modern proverb alluding to this episode of the epic. Here the verb *lòn,* 'to know,' plays an important metaphorical role (see the note for line 369). The well is symbolic of the search for knowledge, down dark walls through the shadows to truth (water). There is no direct path to knowledge, but one must enter the darkness (*dibi*), that is danger, to obtain it. Often the path to knowledge is fraught with contradictions—Who would ever dig a twisted well? How could water be drawn from it? And the seeker is often the object of ridicule, but the acquisition of knowledge results in the acquisition of power, and in the Mande world that is one of the highest valued properties. The use of this proverb in society might imply something like the proverb, "Once bitten, twice shy."

(739ff.) This praise-poem is composed of standard, albeit variant, praise-names for hunters. Here the elder brother is praising the younger for his bravery (see the note for lines 749–51).

(739) *Snake* (blacksmith totem) *and fetish country* suggest the wilderness, and the domain of the hunter who of necessity deals extensively in the occult.

(740) *Stench* of death and danger, companions of those who deal in the occult, are suggested by this line.

(741) *Cutter-of-Fresh-Heart* and *Cutter of-Fresh-Liver.* Allusions to a sort of communion ceremony which takes place over freshly killed game. Hearts and livers, thought by many to contain much occult power (*nyama*), are cooked and shared among the hunters soon after the kill. This traditional gesture exists among many ethnic groups in Africa and Arabia, not necessarily accompanied by a folk belief.

(742–43) *King-of-the-Wilderness.* Past the boundary (*dankun*) of the village, one enters the wilderness, domain of danger and *fa-denya* (see note for lines 356–59). This praise-name carries the connotation of a hero of great strength and control over the occult.

Kininbi and *Kalinka* are obscure.

(744–48) Standard formulaic style of presenting opposites common in Mande poetry. Town dwellers have no power in the bush, and hunters are powerless in the town.

(749–51) Etiological legend explaining the origin of the surname Jabagatè, a clan of casted bards, based on a folk etymology of its syllables. *Jè,* 'to reject' is suffixed with *-baga,* 'agent/ER.' *Tè* is a negative marker. Though incorrect grammatically, it was explained to me that the implied meaning is: 'There is no refuser'; i.e. one who would refuse to reward the bard after his praises were sung could not be found.

(752) *Sangoyi, the Long-Bow.* Same man as Kala Jula Sangoyi. See note for line 5.

(761) *Kòròkò.* Mande surname.

(770) The person referred to is Massa Makan Diabaté (Jabaatè), then researcher at the Institut des Sciences Humaines du Mali and one of the men who assisted in collecting the epic.

(772) The hunters will use all the items they stack together as tokens of proof that they are the ones who killed the buffalo. Motifs suggested here are H 80, Identification by tokens, and H 111, Identification by garment.

(776) *Lounging platform.* Located at the center of most villages, the lounging platform is the gathering place for the town meetings and often merely the center of local conversation in the evenings.

(794) *Tawulen,* 'royal drum,' from the Arabic word *el-ṭabl.* This word may have ultimately come from a Sanskrit word.

(796) *Like it or not.* The message of the drum, based on an onomatopoeic interpretation of the drum's sound, which is said to resemble the compound verb *ka diya-guya,* 'to be forced/compelled.' In short, drop everything and come to the village square.

(799–800) Motif Q 112, Half of a kingdom as a reward, is suggested by this line.

(802–04) Possibly a proverb, these lines imply that trying to help a leper is a waste of time, for he knows best what he needs. The relevance to the text is obscure.

(824) *Modibo Keyta.* President of the Republic of Mali at the time of the recording of this epic. The following genealogy will help clarify these lines. It is taken from Jean-Marie Kònè, "Portrait et Profil," in his *Les 50 Ans* (Koulouba, Mali: Imprimerie du Mali, cf. 1965): 57–65.

Lamuru Keyta
|
Daba Keyta = Fatuma Kamara
|
Modibo Keyta

(828) *Jire* (Djiré) is the home town of Modibo Keyta. It is located near Nioro du Sahel in the northwest of Mali.

(830–31) The reference here is to transportation by airplane (see line 1233 below).

(833–34) These two lines praising Son-Jara may be used in Modibo's praise-poem, for both are surnamed Keyta. Any familial or ancestral praise-line may be used in a poem celebrating any of the clan's members.

(847) *Tura Magan*. The most illustrious member of the Tarawere clan, the descendant of Dan Manse Wulandin, is here praised in a poem actually recited to a predecessor. Because Tura Magan is considered the greatest Tarawere, his name is used to praise all Taraweres. See note for lines 833–34.

(851ff.) Three motifs are suggested here: B 391, Animal grateful for food; B 421, Helpful dog; and B 422, Helpful cat.

(873–76) The symbol here is that of seduction. A woman's legs spread apart symbolizes her sexual availability. Thus she is taught as a young girl to sit with her legs held tightly together. I have also observed this traditional gesture in Somalia and suspect that it can be found in other parts of Africa.

(880) Motif L 102, Unpromising heroine, is suggested here.

(934) The spittle of a saint or shaman is commonly used as a healing medicine in many parts of Africa and the Middle East. A greeting gesture I once observed in Mali equated spittle with a blessing. Asking the blessing of a bard and diviner, a woman held out her cupped hands before her. The bard audibly spit into her hands, though the act was symbolic, for there was no moisture involved in the gesture. The woman then wiped her face with her hands, symbolically bathing her face with the blessing. I have also observed actual and symbolic spitting in Amhara and Oromo greetings in Ethiopia. In Mali incantations over various libations are generally terminated by spitting into the mixture before it is consumed. The moisture of the spittle vitalizes the power of the brew.

(950–61) The reference is to social custom. Elder brothers usually marry first, and the family's wealth goes to furnish him with bridewealth. Younger brothers must wait their turn. This tradition is also suggestive of Motif T 131.2, Younger child may not marry before elder.

(965) *Lelelele.* Idiophone, possibly representing the passage of time.

(968) *Seek pleasure and duty,* literally 'to seek *sunnah* and *farila* with her.' Reference to Islamic marriage law. The *sunnah* ('custom/use') is composed of revelations and articles of faith recorded after the completion of the Koran and may be the most important source of doctrine next to that book. The term *farila* is obscure, but I was told that it is another source of Moslem law. Islamic law speaks of sexual intercourse as a man's duty to his wife as well as his pleasure, and it is this point that is implied in this line.

(972) *Bilililili.* Idiophone for the sound of Sugulun stretching out her body.

(1010–14) The meaning of these so-called ancient greetings is obscure. They are often quoted in epic poetry in variant forms, but they are not commonly used today.

(1028) *Nakana Tiliba.* A great sorceress, the head of the nine Queens-of-Darkness, about whom the plot will later speak (see below lines 1937ff.).

(1031) *Bilal.* See note for line 173.

(1033) *Token.* This talisman or amulet is very powerful and full of *barakah,* 'grace/power.'

(1034–37) This episode is described as preordained and foretold.

(1051–52) In other words, the struggle for birthright and inheritance.

(1060) The old women excuse their neglect to deliver the message with this expression (i.e., one should prepare oneself).

(1063) *Tumu Maninya.* Legendary female bard who is said to have invented the musical instrument called the iron rasp (*karinya, nkarinya, karanya, ŋarinya, ŋarinyè*), a cylindrical musical instrument split open from one end to the other and grooved along each side of the split. A metal wire is used to play the iron rasp, either by "rasping" the cylinder along the grooves or by clanging it on either end.

(Between 1072 & 1073) The bard took a break at this point in the performance, after about one and a half hours of singing. When he resumed, he took up the plot further on, beyond the point where he left it. Such gaps are common in oral recitations and are hardly noticed by the audience, most of whom are thoroughly acquainted with the plot. In the transformation from oral to written styles, however, such gaps can be disturbing, particularly to an audience foreign to the story. For clarification the missing plot has been inserted in prose, but the line numbering of the poetry remains consecutive.

(1076) *Bèrè-bèrè-bèrè.* Idiophone for dryness.

(1080) *Woman.* Error; the bard means women.

(1082) *Those-Caught-by-their-Craws.* Pejorative name for the old women. It is somewhat misleading to give the name praise-poetry to a genre which also includes a rich tradition of pejorative names.

(1084) *Bòkòlen.* Idiophone for great noise.

(1097) It would be very unusual for two co-wives to be confined in the same hut. The bard has probably put them together for literary reasons, especially for the next episode concerning how the boys get their names.

(1119) *Lucky Karunga.* Praise-(or pejorative) name for Sugulun Kòndè. The meaning is obscure.

(1125) *Ba.* We translated *ba,* 'mother,' here as grandmother to avoid confusion. The old woman is the mother of Fara Magan the Handsome.

(1139) *All hair!* See the note for line 1. Jata, which means 'lion,' is covered with hair at birth, signifying his destiny as a ruthless hero. Motif F 521.1, Man covered with hair like animal, is suggested here. Another interesting occurrence of this motif is in Genesis 25:25, where Esau (meaning 'covering'), whose younger brother Jacob "stole" his birthright from him, is described as covered with hair at birth.

(1152) *Holy-man.* See note for line 274.

(1165) *Ḥājj.* The Moslem pilgrimage to Mecca.

(1166) *Kaabah.* Center of the pilgrimage to Mecca, the *Ka<u>ʕ</u>bah* is a large square building, covered with a big black cloth, and containing a sacred stone. Certain religious ceremonies are performed in and around the *Ka<u>ʕ</u>bah* during the season of the *ḥājj.*

(1178) *Dònba.* See note for line 171.

(1180) *Retreat.* A 27-day isolation, or retreat (*kaluwa*), during which time the diviner performs his duties. Food and drink are brought to him, but he may not see or speak with anyone. When someone has been absent from his friends for a while, he is jokingly asked, *I tun bè kaluwa la wa*?, 'Have you been on retreat?'

(1181) In other words, from performing divination so often.

(1187–89) *Rams.* The symbolism here is that black represents darkness, a major symbol for sorcery. White represents daylight, the state of being known. The blackheaded ram, of course, wins, for its power is greater. This sign is taken as a foretelling of Son-Jara's ascendency to the throne.

(1189) *Dankaran Tuman.* Son-Jara's elder brother's name. He is the Bèrete woman's son.

(1197–98) *Knowing never fails,* etc. Proverb used in praise-proverb mode; in other words, everything becomes known in its proper time.

(1208) *Kong.* Town in northern Ivory Coast, on the west side of the Komoé National Park.

(1212) The potion is for healing the dog's sore mouth.

(1244) The allusion here is to a meeting (probably a political rally) in Dakar in which the bard touched Modibo Keyta, then president of Mali, in the crowd.

(1247) *Disperser-of-Women.* Praise-name for Modibo's mother, emphasizing her beauty and/or power.

(1283) *An d'an yèrè sòrò,* 'We have found our freedom/independence.' This phrase is idiomatic and translates literally, 'We have found ourselves.'

(1292) *Couscous.* A type of cracked millet in West Africa.

(1295) The leaves of the baobab tree are used in making a tasty sauce.

(1302) *Bilika.* Idiophone for the sound of falling tears.

(1311ff.) *King of Nyani,* etc. Elsewhere, this praise-poem is ascribed to Nyani Mansa Kara (Kuru), another legendary figure in Mande tradition. Variation of this type, which might be termed "floating praise-poetry," is common in Mande folklore. Another example is the praise-poem called *Janjon,* which is ascribed to more than one hero (see notes for lines 1813–28 and 1844–58).

Two other themes in Mande folklore are of interest in this respect. The envy of a praise-poem, which sometimes leads the envier to slay and "steal" the poem for himself, and the use of praise-poetry as payment for services rendered or promised may be isolated. The latter theme, for example, is said to be the manner in which the praise-poem called *Duga* came to be sung for the illustrious Bamana king of Segu, Da Monson Jara.

(1311) *Nyani.* See note for line 505.

(1327) *Thickener.* Any foodstuff, such as okra, which makes a sauce sticky and gooey. *Black Lele.* Ceratotheca sesamoides.

(1343) This sentence translates literally, 'He arrived between upness and downness.'

(1345) It is understood here and in line 1362 that the iron bar is not strong enough to hold Son-Jara up.

(1368) Son-Jara defines his failure to rise as his mother's affair, for the spiritual world is her concern. He instructs her to seek more help. Not enough has yet been done to circumvent the Berete woman's curses.

(1372) *Jònba* (also *sunsun,* glossed in folk etymology as 'origin of origins'), 'custard apple tree' (Diospyros mespiliformis). Oaths are frequently sworn over custard apple branches in Mande society and reported in folklore. Other traditions based upon its occult power also exist. For example, if an elderly person becomes ill somewhere outside his/her compound, he/she may be given a custard apple branch for a staff. Not only may it be leaned upon but it is believed by some that strength is gleened from the occult power in the staff. In this manner the ill person may gain enough strength to return home where he/she may die in peace. It is this belief in the occult power of the custard apple branch that is reflected in its use as a staff for Son-Jara's rising in line 1410.

(1395–96) In other words, the woman swears her oath on her virginity at marriage and fidelity afterwards.

(1412) *Clasped his legs.* Traditional gesture for greeting a hunter hero.

(1424) *Danka.* Idiophone, the meaning of which is obscure.

(1425) *Kapok* and *Flame* trees grow tall and straight. The image may be a comparison of Son-Jara's legs with these trees.

(1436) *Tunyu Tanya.* Idiophone, the meaning of which is obscure, but some assistants thought it suggested the gait of walking or swaying from side to side, albeit with force.

(1441–45) In other words, muddy water (Dankaran Tuman) cannot be compared to pure water (Son-Jara). The idiophone *wasili* is obscure and lines 1444 and 1445 were inaudible on the tape.

(1479) *Yrrrrr.* Idiophone for the sound of a surging crowd.

(1484–87) In other words, the reason Son-Jara walks today cannot be "known" and counteracted through sorcery, for Son-Jara's occult power is now too strong.

(1528) *Gejebu.* Idiophone for the sound of Son-Jara's mother kneeling on the ground.

(1540) *The tail* of wild game is considered strong in occult power (*nyama*) and is often kept as a trophy. It is also used in conjury. By giving the trophy to the elder, Son-Jara is acknowledging his elder brother's birthright in spite of the pronouncement of his father, who, incidentally, is not mentioned again in the epic. The rivalry, however, has gone too far to be reversed now.

(1553) *Ma'an.* Contraction of Magan.

(1575) *Safo-dog.* A favorite sacrifice, but its exact nature is obscure. The dog is considered an animal possessed of extraordinary occult power.

(1581–82) It is unusual to restrain a dog so thoroughly. The viciousness of the dog symbolizes the ruthlessness of its owner.

(1586) This line was a false start.

(1593) *Causer-of-Loss.* Praise-name for Son-Jara, emphasizing his ruthlessness.

(1594–95) These lines imply that it is usual to restrain a cow in such a fashion, but unusual to so restrain a dog.

(1602) *Tomorrow's Affair.* Symbolic of Son-Jara's coming to power in the future.

(1608) *Fèsè fèsè fèsè.* Idiophone for the sound of the dog ripping the flesh of the other dog.

(1617) The "something" is strong occult power.

(1619) *Younger-Leave-Me-Be.* Symbolic of the elder's fear that his younger brother will usurp his power.

(1620) *Sin-ji tègè,* 'to sever the bonds of family'; literally, 'to cut off breast milk.' See note for line 418.

(1652) *Tail.* An insulting pun, meaning leave at once.

(1653–54) *Sugulun Kulunkan* and *Manden Bukari* are Son Jara's full siblings (*ba-denlu*). He therefore has no traditional rivalry with them as he does with Dankaran Tuman, his half-brother (*fa-den*).

(1657) In other words, I will chop through your neck so hard that an ax or sword will bury itself in the ground the length of a hand span before it comes to a halt.

(1671) *The Kuyatè matriarch* is the female bard Tumu Maniya. See note for line 1063.

(1692) *They* are the followers of Dankaran Tuman.

(1699) *Karanga.* Obscure name. Jobi, the Seer (line 1701) is said to have been from the Kònatè clan.

(1703–15) A digression which alludes to an etiological legend unknown to the assistants. It appears to concern the founding of the town of Bisandugu which is in Guinea near Sananko, where Samory Ture was born.

(1708) Line obscure on tape. For Mount Genu, see note for line 218.

(1718ff.) *Tulunbèn,* King of the region of Kolè with its capital at Sigiri in modern northeast Guinea, is an ancestor of the Magasubaa clan.

(1740–45) The motivation for this sacrifice is obscure but may involve Son-Jara's need for a powerful sacrifice to protect him on his next stopover with the sorceresses. Note that the drastic sacrifice destroys King Tulunbèn, but does not harm the more powerful hero Son-Jara. Again, the violation of tabu by a hero is done to gain occult power.

(1749) *Arakan* (*arkān* in Arabic), 'litany'; literally, 'pillar of faith,' of which ritual prayer (*ṣalāh, ṣalāt*) is one of five. The litany (*ar-raga'ah*) is the first part of each daily prayer, which is what the bard is referring to here.

(1765) *Fikiri,* possibly 'Place-of-the-Bound.' Name of a lake.

(1766) Obscure passage, possibly alluding to an old form of public punishment similar to dunking.

(1778) Note abrupt change of scene. We are transported back to the Manden and the affairs of King Dankaran Tuman.

(1780) *Ta-Suma-Gani-Latè,* 'Caress-of-Hot-Fire,' appears to be a praise-name for King Dankaran Tuman's daughter, emphasizing her sexual appeal.

(1781) *Dòka the Cat* is Son-Jara's royal bard, usurped by Dankaran Tuman when he exiled Son-Jara.

(1782) *Susu Mountain Sumamuru Kantè.* Sorcerer king of the country of Susu, casted blacksmith, scourge of Islam, and archenemy of Son-Jara.

(1786) *Balaphone.* Musical instrument resembling the xylophone. The keys are made of rosewood, and calabashes of different sizes tied below the keys provide resonance. Players often attach metal jinglers to their hands which resonate when the keys are struck with mallets. The word balaphone is a combination of the Mandekan word *bala* and the English suffix -phone.

(1797) *Dark Forest.* Both words are images of the occult. *Dibi,* 'darkness,' implies the secretive milieu of sorcery, while the forest symbolizes the realm of chaos (see note for lines 356–59). The image is of a pagan sorcerer-king's domain.

(1813ff.) The *Janjon* is a floating praise-poem, sung here for Sumamuru (see the note for lines 1311ff.). This poem is said to be sung to warriors going into battle. (Another praise-poem called the *Duga* is said to be sung to warriors coming out of battle.) Lines 1813–15 are Kantè clan ancestors, while lines 1816–28 are praise-names for Sumamuru, emphasizing his occult power and ruthlessness.

(1825) *King of Yesteryear* (or King of Tradition/Traditional King). Praise-name for Sumamuru strongly suggesting a pagan versus Moslem theme in the epic, with Son-Jara representing the Moslem forces. Some have suggested this theme as the key to understanding the real meaning of the epic. It seems more likely, however, that many other themes are of equal importance. In any case, Islam in Mande tradition syncretized with the pagan forces it fights. See note for lines 325ff.

(1835) The audience acquainted with the legend understands at this point that Sumamuru's occult power enables him to hear his balaphone no matter where he is at the time it is played.

(1837) Sumamuru suspects the bard of being a jinn (see the note for line 103), because Dòka the Cat was able to penetrate and survive Sumamuru's occult world.

(1844–45) *Kukuba,* etc. These four villages are sites of confrontation at which Son-Jara has the upper hand over Sumamuru after the turning point of their struggle. Stylistically they are matched by villages which Son-Jara founds after confrontations in which Sumamuru gains the upper hand (see notes for lines 2636ff).

(1872–74) *Hair shaving.* Part of the Moslem naming ceremony on the eighth day of a child's life. See the note for line 341. Here its use symbolizes rebirth.

(1874) The explanation for this name change is left out of this variant. When it is included, it is an etiological legend based on a folk etymology of the names, thus:

> *bala* = 'balaphone'
> *Fasege,* from *i fasa kè* = 'do your praise'
> *Kuyatè,* from *ku ye an cè* = 'there is a matter between us'

The combination of the names is thus said to mean, 'I praise thee with the balaphone, for there is something between us.' The "something" is the master/bard relationship of a casted man to his patron.

(1883–84) *Vicious dog.* Proverb used as a warning to King Dankaran Tuman. The sense is that if the king kills his own vicious dog (Son-Jara), then another dog (enemy) will attack him.

(1890–91) The reference here is obscure.

(1893–1902) Etiological legend based on a folk etymology. King Dankaran Tuman and his entourage flee the Manden, now coming under Susu sovereignty, and go to live in Guinea. Nzèrèkòrò (or Nzèrèkòrè) is in extreme southwestern Guinea close to the borders of both Liberia and Ivory Coast. According to this legend, the new ethnic name for the people becomes Kisi (line 1899), which is the Maninka verb, 'to be spared.' Actually the Kisi belong linguistically to the West Atlantic family which includes Temne, Wolof, Fulani and Serer. Masanta (line 1900) is about 120 kms. to the north-northwest of Nzèrèkòrò. The surname Gindo (line 1902) is a common name among the ethnic group called Dogon and appears to be out of place geographically since no Kisi families bear this surname. The Dogon live in Mali to the north and east of Bamako.

(1905) *Gourds in mouths.* Although described in this variant as a literal action, the image is one of government censorship and repression. No one was permitted to speak out.

(1910ff.) Son-Jara's journey to and subsequent mastery over the nine Queens-of-Darkness suggests Motif F 81, Descent to lower world of dead, and functions to empower him close to the point of invulnerability. Many praise-names also emphasize the ruthlessness of the stock Mande hero figure, especially as a violator of tabu. By surviving the release of occult power caused by violating a tabu, the hero gains control over that power. Accomplishing this task is not easy (compare the praise line, 'A man of power is hard to find'), as witnessed by Son-Jara's near miss with the nine witches.

Son-Jara's exile appears to function as a period of strengthening his forces, both military and spiritual, which he must do in order to defeat the strong sorcerer king Sumamuru. The exile, or retreat, in order to gain strength is a common motif in Africa and Arabia.

(1910–11) *Kankira,* etc. These two men are ancestors of the Saginugu clan of blacksmiths.

(1913) *Red bull.* The color of the bull symbolizes the forces of *fa-denya* (see note for lines 356–59).

(1928) Not returning the greeting is a grave insult, emphasizing the extreme antisocial behavior of the witches.

(1935ff.) The sacrifice which these sorceresses will perform needs some explanation. In the traditional theology of many Mande-speaking peoples, the individual is believed to have a spiritual wraith (*ja*), which is located in the body during waking hours. (Moslems and Christians have used the term to mean 'soul.') The wraith may wander out of the body when its master is asleep, and it becomes visible as one's shadow in the sunlight. It is the *ja* which is visible in mirrors and is the image seen in photographs.

The form of conjury these sorceresses practice involves the removal of a person's *ja* from his/her body through occult means. The *ja* is then put into an animal (in this case, the red bull), which is slaughtered and eaten in communion. Once the animal is consumed, there is no possible reversal of the sacrifice. The sorceresses have no trouble regenerating the bull (after all they have power over life and death), but it will be noticed that the conjury is reversed before the communion ceremony takes place.

(1937) *Nakana Tiliba.* The head sorceress may be the same person as Son-Jara's aunt. See line 1028.

(1939) In other words, endless questions only lead to trouble, so do as you are told.

(1967) Motif D 112.1, Transformation: man to lion, is suggested by this line.

(1988) *Custard apple tree.* Sacred tree (see note for line 1372), which will be used in a divination ceremony later. Unfortunately the bard forgot to describe the ceremony at the proper time in the plot. This ceremony will help Son-Jara decide where to go next on his exile. It involves taking the custard apple branch to a fork in the road and striking it on each of the paths in expectation of being shown certain signs, either a spring of blood or milk. The interpretation of these signs exists in variant form. Some bards, such as the late Kèlè Mònsòn Jabaatè of Kita, interpret the milk as representing cosmic balance between *fa-denya* and *ba-denya* (see note for lines 356–59 and for lines 491–94); thus, it is the GO sign. The blood is seen as chaos and imbalance and is interpreted as the STAY sign (see lines 1202–16, pp. 278–79 of Rex Moser, "Foregrounding in the Sunjata, The Mande Epic," Ph.D. dissertation, Indiana University Linguistics Department, 1974). Other bards, such as Fa-Digi's son Magan Sisòkò, interpret blood as the GO sign, presumably because it represents the seeking for power in dangerous places. In this context, milk would represent the static, safe, and weak fortune; thus it would be the STAY sign. Whichever interpretation is used, Son-Jara always gets the GO sign to proceed to the city of Mèma.

(1991) *Jula Fundu*. Place name, obscure to the assistants.

(1992) *Mossi*. A Voltaic people, most of whom live in Upper Volta.

(1995ff.) No motif number could be found for the regeneration of the bull, part by part. However, I know this motif to be traditional, for it provides the basis for several folktales and legends in West Africa. See, for example, the Jabo narrative entitled "The Cow Tail Switch" found on pp. 85–88 of Harold Courlander, *A Treasury of African Folklore* (New York: Crown Pubs., Inc., 1975).

(2002) *Knots* are used in many amulets, or they are tied into the strings which hold them, in order to strengthen the efficacy of the amulet. Amulets with knotted strings attached to them are called *tafo*.

(2005) *Kitibili Kintin*. Incantation, the meaning of which is obscure.

(2015–16) *Messenger*. A formula divorcing the messenger from the responsibility of the content of his message. Traditionally, messengers have an immunity from any bad news contained in their messages. The formula is needed because the tabu of harming the messenger may be violated like any other tabu.

(2020ff.) Son-Jara sends the messenger back to Sumamuru with veiled messages (some are proverbs) as warnings.

(2021–22) *Friday milk*. When shepherds care for the herds of others, payment for their services may include the milk drawn on Friday, the holy day. Milk from any other day may not be offered for sacrifice, because it is not the shepherd's to give. With this proverb, Son-Jara warns Sumamuru that he may not rule the Manden for it is not his "Friday milk."

(2023–24) Proverb. The *wet nurse* is Sumamuru and the child is the

Manden. In other words, Sumamuru may rule the Manden temporarily, but it will never be his child to keep.

(2025) The image of the elder as king belongs to Son-Jara, although he was not the first-born.

(2040) *Dugunò*. Clan name.

(2042) *Sigi game*. Variant explanations exist for this game. The one described in this text seems to be the modern game of *npari,* or *nperi* (see note for line 2046), and *sigi* is described as the "ancestor" of modern games. The bard describes their development in terms of a genealogy. The most detailed variant explanation for *sigi* I found came from the late bard Wa Kamisòkò from Kirina. He defined *sigi fili* as 'casting out doubt,' and described it as an ancient test whereby combatants in Old Mali gave proof of their genealogy. Those warriors too close in kinship, or who belonged to clans which had sworn alliances, were not permitted to fight each other.

The game was described as follows. The two adversaries came together over a large pot of boiling potash (*sègè-kata*). Large metal bracelets (*sigi-nègè*) were then put into the boiling potash. Next the two men recited their genealogies and swore they spoke the truth. The test came when they cast their hands into the boiling potash. If a hand was burned before its owner could get the bracelet on, he was lying. If no kinship existed, the warriors were free to face each other on the battle field, but because so much occult power was released during the test, only one weapon could slay the pair tested in the *sigi* game. The special bullet (*sigi-nègè-den*) is cylindrical in shape and measures about one-half inch long. These metal objects are available for sale in most modern markets today for use in occult preparations which market sellers refused to explain to me.

The function of the *sigi* game in this text is obscure, because it is not clear who sent Kabala Simbon to Mèma with it. If sent by Son-Jara's enemies, it would appear to be a way of tricking him into erring so that his occult power might be circumvented and his demise assured. If sent by his supporters or potential future subjects, the function would be different. Other texts, for example the Kèlè Mònsòn variant mentioned in the note for line 1988, treat the *sigi* game as an ordeal of wisdom, applied to Son-Jara in order to determine his worthiness to become king.

(2045) *Wori* (*Woli, Wari*). The familiar African (Caribbean, South Asian) game of shifting tokens from one of twelve or more holes to the next. Many variants of this game exist all over the world, and the game often goes by the generic name derived from Arabic, "Mankala." For a good description of the African variants, see Claudia

Zaslavsky, "The Game Played by Kings and Cowherds—and Presidents, Too!" in her *Africa Counts* (Boston: Prindle, Weber & Schmidt, 1973): 116–36.

(2046) *Pari* (*npari, nperi*). Try as I might, I could never quite grasp the rules of this popular Malian game. It is played on a mound of sand (or dirt), upon which a set of geometric designs is drawn. Pairs of sticks are put into position alternately by two players. In the second part of the game, the players begin to move and jump opposing sticks, sometimes with one stick, sometimes with the pair. The player who eliminates his opponent's sticks (or a certain number of them) wins.

(2077) This line is a false start.

(2093ff.) *Watarawaa,* etc. The ritualistic phrases the Prince must recite. The meanings of *watarawaa* and *nderen* are obscure.

(2106ff.) *Watarawaa,* etc. The ritualistic answer that Son-Jara must properly pronounce in response to the king's challenge. The meanings of *faringa, nkuramè* and *jòn jòn jòn* are obscure.

(2203) *Like it or not.* See note for line 796.

(2204) *Tabule.* Variant of *Tawulen.* See note for line 794.

(2232) Error, which the bard corrects on the next line. Kankuba Kantè would have been kin to Sumamuru.

(2233–34) *Sugulun Kòndè.* Error by the bard, who means Sugulun Kònatè. Son-Jara's sister who is also called Sugulun Kulunkan in this variant. The increasing number of errors would suggest that the bard is getting tired.

(2235ff.) The image of Sugulun tearing off the gourds (see note for line 1905) symbolizes the use of her sorcery to give the Manden rebels power to take action independent of Sumamuru's control. From this point in the epic, it is Son-Jara's sister who inherits the status of supporting sorceress from her mother. Also from this point we witness the growth of Son-Jara's occult power and the weakening of Sumamuru's.

(2237) *Sara* (*Sira, Sita*) *Fada* (*Fara*). Ancestor of the Jawara ethnic group, this bard later accompanies Tura Magan in the conquest of the Gambia (see below, lines 3024ff.). According to one variant, Tura Magan gave Sara Fada the golden throne of the Dark King of Jòlòf.

Around 1964, an event in Mali occurred which was a direct result of this legend. A group of Jawaras, who had long since migrated to the sacred city of Kaaba (Kangaba) near the border with Guinea and Mali, converted to Islam. I was told that at that time, they melted down a large object of gold and sold it on the open market. Elders of this group explained that this object had been the throne of the Dark King of Jòlòf. It was reported that the melting was done because they feared use of the throne as a pagan fetish. This event has become the basis of a large body of variant legends. Another version, for example, claimed that the object was Tura Magan's spear or sword, which was cut up, divided among its caretakers, and sold in the gold market in Bamako, after which I assume it was melted down.

(2238) *Those people* are the Manden rebels.

(2260) *Fa-Kandi Tunandi.* This character was obscure to all the assistants.

(2273 & 2276) Error by the bard, same as explained in note for lines 2233–34.

(2275) *Kò-nyina,* 'club rat.' The translation is conjectural here. A *kò-nyina* (literally 'creek rat') lives in swampy areas and around rivers and might be a muskrat.

(2279) In other words, Sugulun extracts the hearts and livers by means of conjuring, not by slaughtering the animals, and transports them back to her kitchen also by use of occult medicine. These highly valued parts are needed to serve to the guests from the Manden.

(2304) *Joma,* etc. Two villages on the Sankaran River in Guinea.

(2308) *Garan.* At this point in the recitation, the bard's naamusayer was replaced by another man named Garan.

(2360) The dishonor mentioned would have been not having sustenance for the guests.

(2369) In other words, his verbal abuse and bad temper are enough to release sufficient occult power to blow off his sister's dress. This act is a symbol of her public embarrassment.

(2377) *Hamina.* Place name, obscure to all the assistants.

(2396ff.) The bard digresses to self praise. Massa Makan (see the note for line 770) had asked *Fa-Digi* to make a recording for the national radio station.

(2403) The reference here is to the request for this performance of the epic. The white man is Charles S. Bird, who collected the text.

(2411) *Se,* 'shea tree.' See note for lines 356–59.

(2420ff.) *Ah, God,* etc. An incantation to rejuvenate the shea tree. Note the religious syncretism in this episode. The God of Islam is consulted for materials needed to sacrifice to a pagan fetish.

(2443) *Change dwelling.* Euphemism for death; i.e. 'let me die.'

(2451) Son-Jara prepares his mother and buries her in secret because of her powerful sorcery. Grave robbing, I was told, was common in Mali, especially because a powerful person's fetishes are sometimes buried with him/her, and the site may be treated as a shrine. One such shrine near Kirina is believed to be that of Son-Jara himself, though similar claims are made in other parts of Mali and Guinea.

(2464–65) The reason the people of Mèma wanted payment for the land is obscure. One assistant suggested that they may have wished to discourage Son-Jara from burying his mother in their land for fear that leaving her behind might constitute grounds for a claim to the throne of Mèma.

(2475) *Sigi-nègè,* 'cornerstone fetish.' I am not sure if this object is the same as the one mentioned in the note for line 2042. The reference may be to the *sigi-nègè-den* mentioned in the same note.

(2486–90) This passage is obscure, and has given rise to several variant transcriptions, the most reasonable of which is translated here.

(2513) In other words, this "payment" is a veiled message of warning from Son-Jara to Prince Burama. Note that the list of items put into the bag does not exactly match the list of items spilled out of the bag. This type of inconsistency is very common in epic poetry.

(2534) Note that in public Son-Jara is actually burying a log. (See note for line 2451.)

(2535ff.) This part of the epic is suggestive of motif L 111.1, Exile returns and succeeds.

(2557ff.) *Dabò,* from *a d'a bò,* 'he pulled it off.' Etiological legend of the origin of the Dabò clan based on a folk etymology of its name. In this text, the Dabò is a casted man. To be thrown by a casted man is an insult to Son-Jara's honor, thus the reaction from Tura Magan.

(2578) *Sòmònò,* boatman. Not an ethnic or clan name, but a group of clans among the Mande-speakers, who earn their living on the rivers as fishermen and transporters, or who are considered to have originated in this profession. Among the Bamana, the Sòmònò are not casted.

(2636ff.) The founding of these towns is symbolic of Son-Jara's failure to defeat Sumamuru, whose occult remains stronger than Son-Jara's at this point. Note that each village is celebrated in a praise-poem which plays upon the meaning of its name. See also the note for lines 1844–45.

(2689) The seduction of Sumamuru by Son-Jara's sister is suggestive of motif N 476, Secret of unique vulnerability disclosed.

(2699ff.) At this point Sumamuru begins to disclose the secrets of his sacrifice for control over the Manden. I am not certain of the sacrifice metaphor here.

(2723) In other words, he severs his relationship with her. See note for line 418.

(2727) Sumamuru's mother disowns him as well, cutting off another part of his occult strength and weakening him further.

(2731ff.) The reference here is to a custom of marriage. There is a tradition which requires a wife to return to her parents' house after one week of marriage for a final visit and to get her dowry. When she marries, part of her dowry are her *minèn-kolon,* 'useful containers.' This collection is composed of calabashes and other containers and stirring devices, such as the calabash spoon Sugulun mentions. A small *minèn-kolon* is considered disgraceful. Sugulun uses this custom as a trick to escape to Son-Jara's camp.

(2753) Fa-Koli's wife is a powerful sorceress; thus Sumamuru envies and steals her from his nephew. In this variant, the theft of his wife drives Fa-Koli into Son-Jara's camp, and further weakens the Susu king, while strengthening Son-Jara.

(2755ff.) *Let the fonio increase,* etc. Incantation said over the food to cause it to increase.

(2758) *Groundpea,* also called Bambara pea (Voandzia subterranea).

(2765–66 & 2768–69) Lines unfortunately obscure on the tape. It was probably here that Sumamuru stole Fa-Koli's wife, and Fa-Koli abandoned his uncle Sumamuru.

(2770) Praise-names for Fa-Koli.

(2796) *Caress-of-Hot-Fire.* See note for line 1780.

(2844) *Kukuba.* See the notes for lines 1844–45 and 2637ff.

(2862) *Kulu-Kòrò.* Village about 50 kms. northeast of Bamako on the Niger River. The name is said to mean 'Under-the-Mountain,' and its origin is said to be connected to this legend. Sumamuru is finally defeated here, and, according to one legend, he disappeared into a cave "under the mountain" near the village.

(2883) *Nyònyòwu.* Idiophone for the sound of Sumamuru drying up. Note the implication that weapons could never harm him, even in his hour of death, for his occult power was too strong for weapons.

(2884) *Nyanan,* 'sacred fetish.' This fetish is still revered and is thought by its disciples to be served by the spirit of Sumamuru. The fetish is a globe-shaped stone, which has carved interlacing diamond patterns on its surface. Chicken feathers and kola nuts were in evidence when I visited the fetish, which is served by a priest of the Kulubali clan and protected by members of the Jara clan who are in the majority in Kulu-Kòrò. I was told that the fetish is consulted for many reasons, among them barrenness in women.

(2889) *Stranger,* etc. Praise-name for Son-Jara, emphasizing his ruthlessness. The image is that he is a stranger in a village in the morning, and by the afternoon he has conquered it and become its chief.

(2930) *Serew.* Idiophone for the sound of the balaphone being put on Mansa Sama's head.

(2942) *Jon jon.* Idiophone, the meaning of which is obscure.

(2949–50) Son-Jara sends these two men on a trading mission to buy horses in the Gambia.

(2957) *Dark Jòlòf.* Kingdom of the Wolof ethnic group who live in modern Senegal and Gambia. The dark image is related to the occult.

(2960) Exchanging the horses for dogs is an insult to Son-Jara.

(2974) One of the self-stated functions of bards is to spur men on to heroic deeds. This function does not always please the men they encourage.

(2985–91) Note that the bard grows weary, and a few lines falter here.

(3006-07) Tura Magan lies alive in his grave as a symbol of his grief. As a result, Son-Jara gives the army to him, and he gains his most well-known praise-name, *su-sare-jòn,* 'Slave-of-the-Tomb' (see line 3025).

(3016–22) *Bugu Turu,* etc. Praise-poem to the Tarawere clan of Tura Magan, emphasizing the strength of its genealogy. The names are Tarawere ancestors, all of whom are obscure, except the last one. *Makan-taa* is the Mande term for ḥājji, 'Moslem pilgrim.' Some claim that this man brought secrets back from his pilgrimage to Mecca with which he founded the Komo Society in Mali. Again, we can see the syncretism of Moslem and non-Moslem religious elements.

(3031) *Passage-of-Tura-Magan.* A ford either on the Baoulé River near Kita or on the Faleme River which divides modern Mali and Senegal. Both rivers are tributaries of the Senegal River.

(3040–43) This passage usually gets a laugh from the audience. The image is that the Jawara bard puffs out his cheeks and slaps them rhythmically with his hands to make a kind of percussion instrument with which to awaken the king in the mornings.

The agitator compares the musical richness of the Gambia at that time to the musical poverty of the Manden and concludes that the Maninkas will lose in battle. We have seen that musical instruments are sometimes associated with the occult (cf. Sumamuru's magic balaphone which he could hear from anywhere in his kingdom). Moreover, music and song stir men's souls to bravery in the Manden as elsewhere, but in the Manden many believe they are possessed of occult power.

(3049 & 3050) *Ford-of-the-frightened-Braves.* Folk etymology accompanied by an etiological legend (lines 3030–50) explaining the origin of the name of this river ford. It might be mentioned here that river-fording legends constitute a major subtype in Mali, and I have collected several of them.

(3053) *Dog-running.* Usually applied to hunters, this praise line is here a play on words. Tura Magan ironically alludes to the insulting swap of horses for dogs (lines 2958–61), while implying that he was merely hunting for pleasure.

(3055) *Nyani Mansa Kara* is the king alluded to here. He is one of many kings said to have fallen under the onslaught of Son-Jara's empire. The praise-poem in lines 1311–24 and 2311–20 is often ascribed to this monarch, and it is sometimes said that Fa-Koli "stole" the praise-poem *Janjon* from Nyani Mansa Kara by defeating him in battle (see note for lines 1813ff.).

(3058 & 3060) *Sanumu* and *Ba-dugu.* Obscure villages (kingdoms?) in the Gambia.

(3063–66) Possibly a reference to the laterite rock in much of the Gambia; it seems reasonable to classify this explanation as a folk etymology.

(3070–72) *Njop* (also spelled Ndiop, Diop). Jocular folk etymology, utilizing a pun. Njop is a common surname in Senegal and the Gambia, and the poet defines it as an onomatopoeic word derived from the sound of Tura Magan's ax chopping (njopping) off Dark Jòlòf King's head.

(3074) *Sane* and *Mane.* Ruling Niancho clans in the Gambia.

(3080) *Golden sword and throne.* Tura Magan gives them to the Jawaras. See the note for line 2237.

Genealogy Charts

A. The Sons of Adam (Hadama-Dinlu)

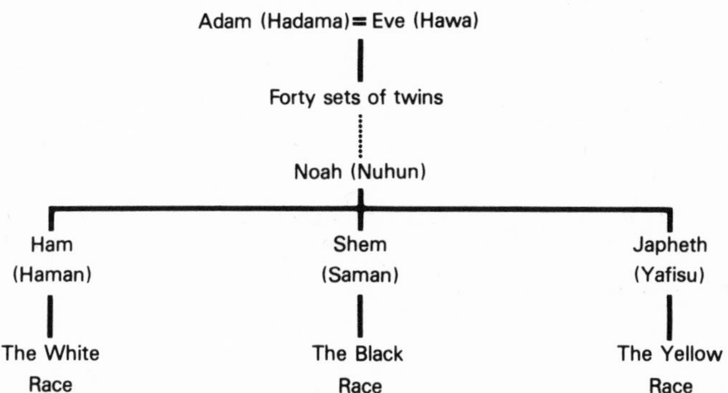

B. The Kònatè Line

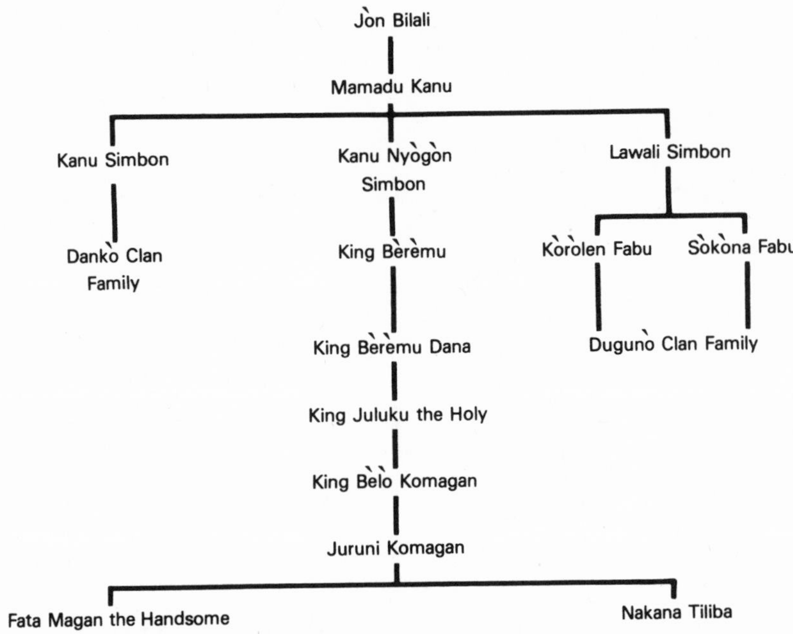

C. The Jawara Line

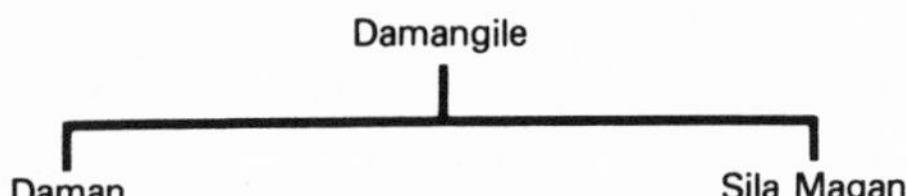

D. The Tunkara Line

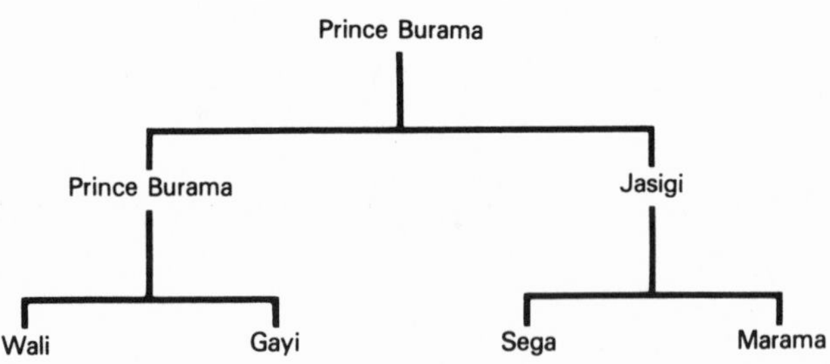

E. Son-Jara's Family

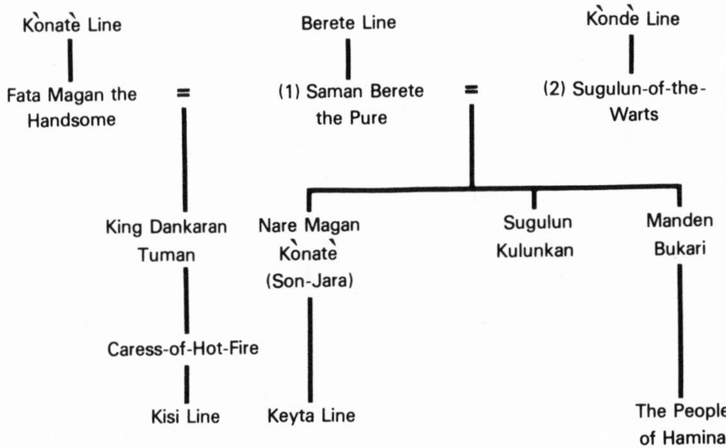

F. The Descendants of Mamuru

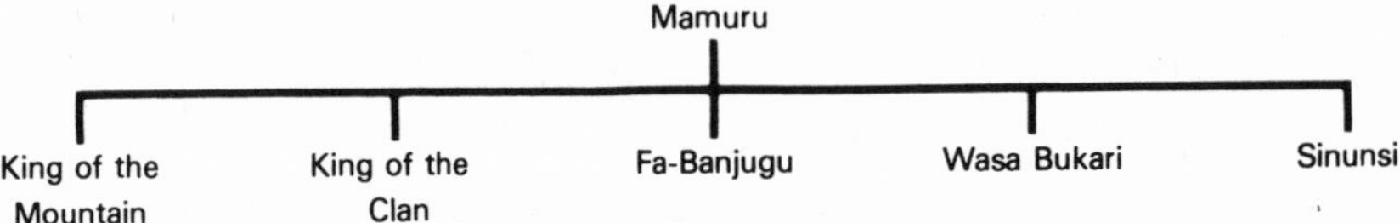

G. The Quraysh Line

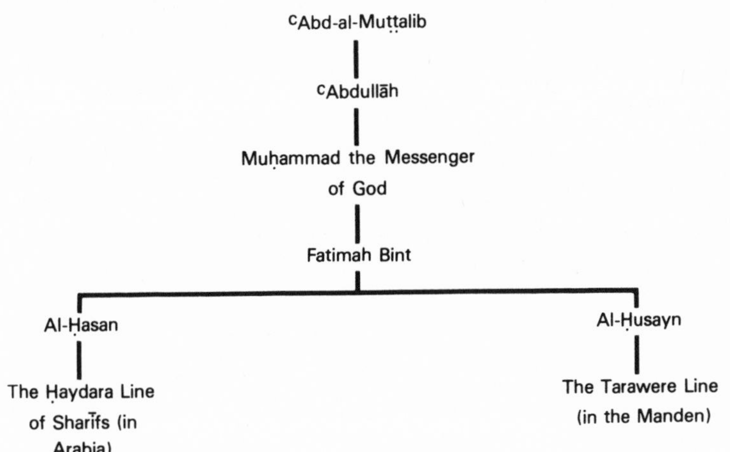

H. The Tarawere Line

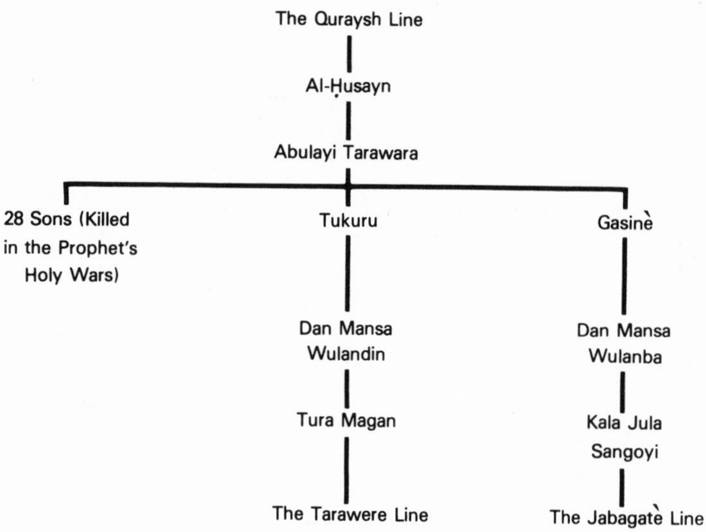

I. The Kòndè (Kònè, Jara) Line

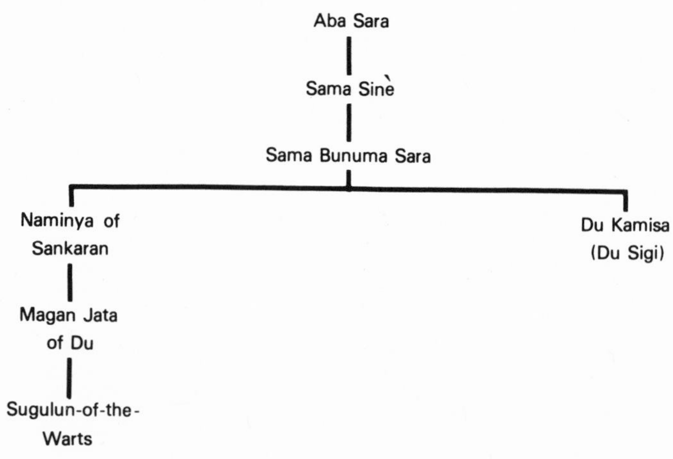

J. The Jabagatè (Jabaatè) Line

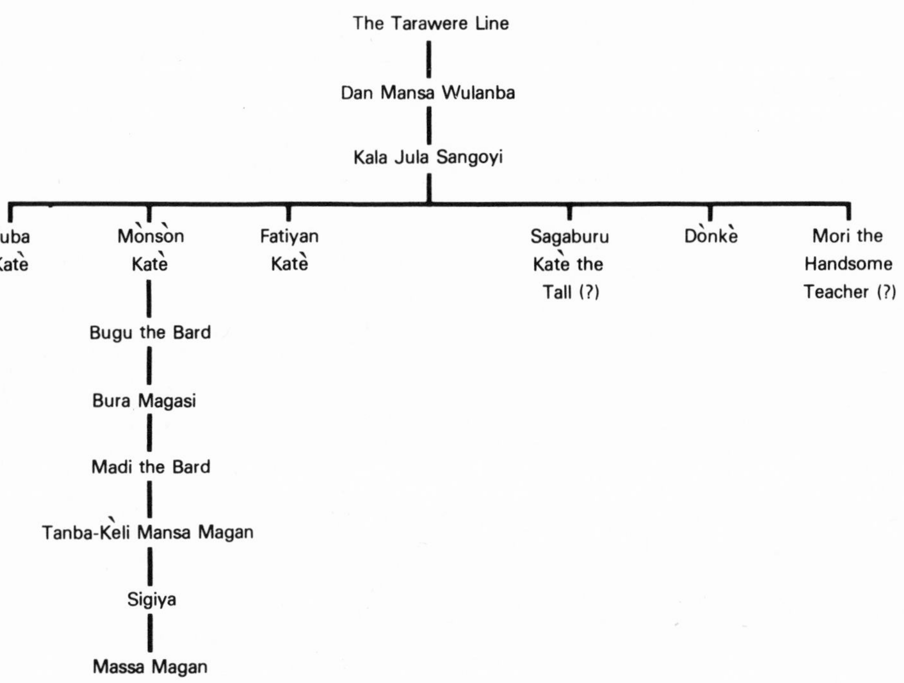

K. The Kantè Line

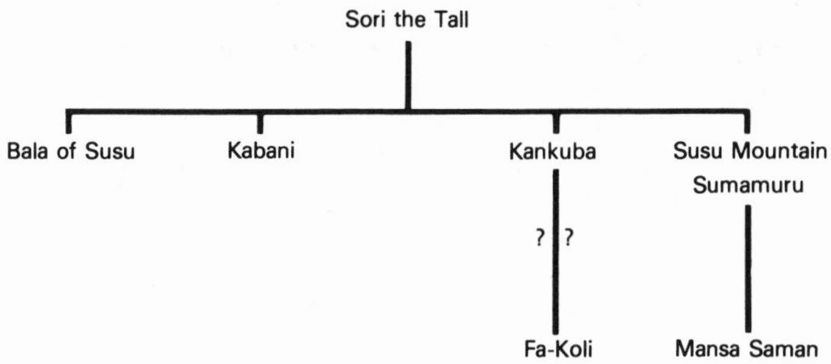

L. The Kuyatè Line

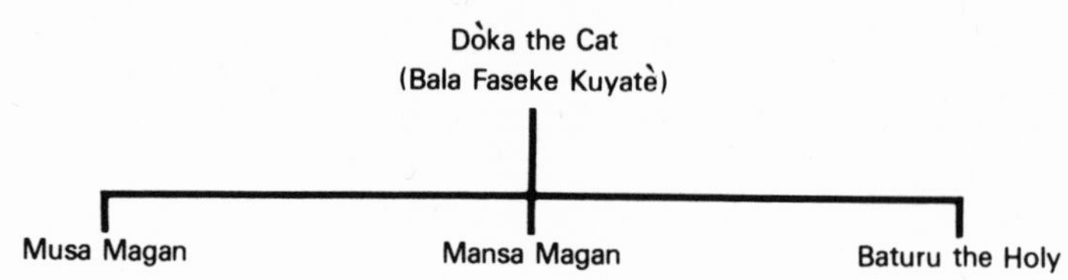

M. The Karangè People

BIBLIOGRAPHY

One of the most interesting aspects of oral literature is the existence of variant forms, for each time the epic is sung, it is different to some degree from the last time it was sung, even by the same bard. A change of region will bring about even more dramatic changes, for the differences in the local social and political setting will be reflected in the variant of the epic recited in that region. The interested reader may want to investigate these changes by reading other versions of the epic of Son-Jara. As far as I am aware, the following bibliography is a definitive list of all the complete variants of this epic that have been published to date. I have divided the list into categories according to the manner of translation. Linear (word-for-word) translations in poetic form are listed in category I, while reconstructed translations, which have been "rewritten" in prose form in the words of the translator or editor, are listed in category II.

I. Linear Translations

Cissé, Youssouf Tata, and Wâ Kamissoko. *La grande geste du Mali des origines à la fondation de l'empire.* Paris: Éditions Karthala et Arsan, 1988.

———. *Soundjata, la gloire du Mali (La grande geste du Mali—Tome 2).* Paris: Éditions Karthala et Arsan, 1988.

Diabaté, Massa Makan. *L'aigle et l'épervier, ou la geste de Sunjata.* Paris: Édition Pierre Jean Oswald, 1975.

Innes, Gordon. *Sunjata: Three Mandinka Versions.* London: School of Oriental and African Studies, University of London, 1974.

Johnson, John William, et al. *The Epic of Son-Jara according to Magan Sisòkò.* Bloomington: Folklore Publications Group, 1979.

Kamissoko, Wâ (trans. and ed. Youssouf Tata Cissé). *L'empire du Mali.* Paris: Fondation SCOA pour la Recherche Scientifique en Afrique Noire, 1975.

———. *L'empire du Mali (Suite).* Paris: Fondation SCOA pour la Recherche Scientifique en Afrique Noire, 1977.

Kone, Cemogo (trans. Lassana Doucoure and Mme Martal). *Soundiata.* Bamako, Mali and Niamey, Niger: Institut des Sciences Humaines du Mali, and Centre Régionale de Documentation pour la Tradition Orale, 1970.

Moser, Rex. "Foregrounding in the Sunjata, the Mande Epic." Ph.D. dissertation, Indiana University, 1974.

II. Reconstructed Translations

Camara, Laye (trans. James Kirkup). *The Guardian of the Word: Kouma Lafôlô Kouma.* Glasgow: William Collins, 1980.

———(trans. James Kirkup). *The Guardian of the Word: Kouma Lafôlô Kouma.* New York: Vintage Books, 1984.
———. *Le mâtre de la parole: kouma lafôlô kouma.* Paris: Librairie Plon, 1978.
Diabaté, Massa Makan. *Kala Jata.* Bamako: Éditions Populaires, 1970.
Konaré Ba, Adam. *Sunjata: le fondateur de l'empire du Mali.* Abidjan, Côte d'Ivoire: Les Nouvelles Édition Africaines, 1983.
Niane, Djibril Tamsir. *Soundjata, ou l'épopée mandingue.* Paris: Présence Africaine, 1960.
———. *Sundiata: An Epic of Old Mali.* London: Longman, 1989.
Sidibe, Bakare K., comp. and ed. *Sunjata.* Banjul, the Gambia: Oral History and Antiquities Division, Vice-President's Office, 1980.
Spaznikov, G. A. *Sund'jita mandigskij epos.* Moscow: Izd. Hudogestvennaja Literatura, 1963.
Zeltner, Frantz de. "La légende de Soundiata." In his *Contes du Sénégal et du Niger.* Paris: Ernest Laroux, 1913.

JOHN WILLIAM JOHNSON is Associate Professor of Folklore and African Studies at Indiana University and author of two books and numerous articles on Somali and Mande linguistics, music, and folklore, including topics in legend, socio-political poetry, and epic. He is coeditor of *Somalia in Word and Image.*